# THEORY AND DESIGN IN
# THE SECOND MACHINE AGE

FOR WISLARD AND BIM

# THEORY AND DESIGN IN THE SECOND MACHINE AGE

MARTIN PAWLEY

Basil Blackwell

Copyright © Martin Pawley, 1990

First published 1990

Basil Blackwell Ltd
108 Cowley Road, Oxford, OX4 1JF, UK

Basil Blackwell, Inc.
3 Cambridge Center
Cambridge, Massachusetts 02142, USA

British Library Cataloguing in Publication Data
A CIP catalogue record for this book is available from
the British Library.

Library of Congress Cataloging-in-Publication Data
Pawley, Martin.
    Theory and design in the second machine age / Martin Pawley.
        p.    cm.
    Includes bibliographical references.
    ISBN 0–631–15828–6
    1. Architecture—Philosophy.    2. Architectural design.
3. Architecture—England.    4. Architecture, Modern—20th century-
England.    5. Architecture—England—Technological innovations.
I. Title.
NA2500.P385    1990
720'.1'05—dc20    89–38458 CIP


Typeset in 10½ on 13 pt Linotype Bembo by
Wyvern Typesetting Ltd, Bristol
Printed in Great Britain by
Butler and Tanner Ltd, Frome, Somerset

# Contents

# List of Illustrations

# Preface

THIS book began at a crowded opening at the Architectural Association in the autumn of 1985. On exhibition was a collection of framed Beaux-Arts-style renderings which had been drawn to sell, not to form the basis of any building project. Held at the Architectural Association, a school founded by students and run by architects for more than a century, the event eloquently epitomized the total defeat of Modern architecture and the triumph of the revivalist, stylistic academicism that only 20 years before had been the sullen and resentful object of Modern scorn.

It was during the course of this *vernissage* that the first of two exchanges on the subject of this book took place. Seeing Peter Reyner Banham in the crowd, on a visit from his home in California, I told him in the course of conversation that I had always wanted to write a sequel to his 1960 work, *Theory and Design in the First Machine Age*. He replied that he had no objection to this, but he thought the project woefully out of date. 'We are on the sixth or seventh Machine Age now,' he said. I took leave to doubt this, but nothing came out of the conversation except Reyner Banham's clear confirmation that he did not object to the use of a derivative of his own famous title.

Two years later the nucleus of one chapter of *Theory and Design in the Second Machine Age* appeared as an article under my name in the magazine *Architectural Review* under the title 'The Architecture of Technology Transfer' (*AR*, September 1987, pp. 31–9) together with a notice of the forthcoming book. In response to this publication the second exchange occurred. The author received a letter from Peter Reyner Banham in Santa Cruz, dated 23 September 1987, raising various points about the contents of the article. It concluded: 'Needless to say there are long stretches of it with which I do not agree, but I am extremely glad that it has been published and, above all, that you wrote it.'

At the time of writing Banham was already in the grip of the cancer that was to kill him within six months, although I was unaware of this until I received the letter. 'If you have heard that I am at death's door, it isn't strictly true, call it a window of death, quite small but very close,' was what he wrote. I replied to this letter on 2 October 1987 thanking him for his interest and endeavouring to answer some of the points he had raised about the article. I also mentioned some of the problems that I had encountered in writing the book and hoped his illness would soon be over so that he could take up his new position as successor to Henry Russell Hitchcock as Professor of Architectural Theory and History at New York University. To this letter I received no reply but, some time later, I learned the nature of Banham's 'window of death' from other sources. He had returned to London where he died on 18 March 1988 aged 66.

As will be evident to the reader, the volume that has finally emerged from my preoccupation with Banham's book is not an academic study modelled on *Theory and Design in the First Machine Age*, but a personal attempt to address the questions about the relationship between technology and architecture posed in its often-quoted last chapter. Lacking Banham's global reach and European dimension, this book is very Anglo-centric compared to his. Most of the architects whose work is discussed and illustrated here live in England, and many of the buildings described are built in England. In this sense the buildings and architects of England, together with the perhaps untypical pressures and limitations they endure, are made to do a job that a better-travelled and more gregarious author might have based more widely. This is a weakness of *Theory and Design in the Second Machine Age*, as well as a distinguishing feature between the two books. The only justification that I can offer the reader is an observation of Banham's own. To the end of his life he took the view that architecture was 'just one out of dozens of ways of approaching the design of buildings, but it happens to be the one which Western civilization still grants cultural hegemony.' This diagnosis he attributed in his letter to me of 23 September 1987 to the influence of Cedric Price; but in truth he had said it before, at the Folkestone Conference on Experimental Architecture twenty years earlier. I still have my notes from the talk he gave on that occasion, and what he said was: 'We must all remember that architecture is only a cultural solution to the problem of enclosure.' If this is true, then it must be a limitation upon the architects and buildings of England no less than those of anywhere else in the world.

In those short statements, separated by twenty years, I detect something of the realism that underlay Reyner Banham's often criticized 'lack of seriousness' about the expendability of the culture of architecture in the twentieth century, a realism that he generally concealed in his prolific journalism, and seldom addressed directly in his books. Banham was a past master, in his own words, 'at treating heavy stuff with a light touch'. The author has no such ability, but he does believe that it is the same stuff that he is touching.

MARTIN PAWLEY
*Widdicombe, 1989*

# Acknowledgements

THROUGHOUT the time I worked on this book I was privileged to be the architecture critic of *The Guardian* and London correspondent for *Casabella*, as well as writing for other magazines. The writing and travelling that this double life entailed, and the contacts with architects, engineers, developers and academics that it brought about, influenced everything that has finally appeared on these pages. Although they are in no way responsible for the views that are expressed here, I owe special thanks to the following persons: My old principal at the AA, William Allen, whose title, 'Architecture in the Age of Science', I have purloined as a chapter heading; Robert Adam, architect, whose essay 'Tin Gods: Technology and Contemporary Architecture' sets forth brilliantly the case for a synthesis of classical design and advanced materials technology; Nick Grimshaw and Richard Horden, both of whom know more about technology transfer in architecture than I shall ever know; Roger Perrin, who took 'high-tech' design to its practical business limits and proved that, in the end, it just wasn't important, but was still prepared to talk about it; Nick Whitehouse of Terrapin Buildings, who opened my eyes to a lot in 1983; Michael Glickman, president of the McCauley Corporation, for whose insights I am always grateful; Jan Kaplicky, whose single-minded devotion to functional design in architecture – as opposed to postmodern planning officers' hoo-ha – must one day turn the tide of reaction and bring him the kind of challenging commission that he so richly deserves; Peter Davey, for publishing 'The Architecture of Technology Transfer' in the *Architectural Review*; Richard Gott; Colin Boyne; Dan Cruickshank and Frank McDonald; the various editors of *The Architect/RIBA Journal* for allowing me to go on thinking aloud on the magazine's 'PS' page since 1980; Tim Goodfellow for persuading me not to abandon the book; and finally (probably to his surprise) Sherban Cantacuzino who, at a very late stage, politely asked me when the first machine age ended and the second began – a rather fundamental question.

# Illustration Acknowledgements

The publishers would like to thank the following for kindly supplying the illustrations used in this book.

Aerofilms (12); Anglia Television (103); Archigram (64); Architectural Design (71, 72, 73); Architectural Press (1, 2, 6, 17, 24, 25, 34, 43, 54, 62(a) and (b), 70, 81, 90, 102); Author (7, 88, 89); Author's collection (4, 39, 47, 51, 55, 57, 60, 63, 67, 82, 100); Cliff Barden (14, 112); Barratt Homes (50); Bovis Limited (86); Dave Bower (26); Britain on View (BTA/ETB) (11); British Aerospace (85, reproduced by permission); British Cement and Concrete Association (56, reproduced by kind permission); British Petroleum (22); British Steel Corporation (58, 74); Richard Bryant (106); Camera Press (79, 115); Central Electricity Generating Board (96); Martin Charles (23, 59, reproduced by permission); CMW Architects (91); Jeremy Cockayne/Arcaid, Sainsbury's plc (97); Peter Cook (18, 21, 41, 65); Richard Davis (94, 95, both photos by Richard Davis); John Donat Photography (8); Terry Farrell Partnership (108(a)); Fiat Auto SpA (36, 42, reproduced by permission); Dougie Firth (33, 83); Fitzroy Robinson Partnership (92); Foster Associates (37, 104); Future Systems (31, 107); Geoff Goode (32); Michael Hopkins and Partners (27, 28, 29); Richard Horden (87, 105); Keith Horne (78); Hulton Picture Library (110, 113); Hulton Picture Library/UPI/Bettman Archive (109); Hunt Thompson Associates (35(a)); Imperial War Museum, London (20, 38); Eva Jiricna Architects (30, © Peter Cook); London Express News and Feature Services (66); Sasha Lubetkin (19); The Mansell Collection (10, 52, 53, 93); Mercedes-Benz (United Kingdom) (44, 45, 46, reproduced by kind permission); A. Murray (London) Ltd (40, reproduced by kind permission); The MVA Consultancy (84); Nectar Homes (49); Stephen Parker (13); Popperfoto (111); Jo Reid and John Peck (35(b) and 108(b)); Michael Reynolds (101); Rockwool International (98); Rosehaugh Stanhope Developments (114, reproduced by permission. Photo by Sealand Photography); Messrs Scott, Brownrigg and Turner (68, reproduced by permission. Photo by Richard Turpin); Glen Small (75 (line drawing), 76, 77); Stirling Wilford Architects (9); Tanner, Nesselwang (5, © Kurverwaltung Schwangau); Terrapin International Ltd (61, 99); Tribune Media Services (69, reprinted by permission); Winchester Design Associates (48); Charlotte Wood (15, 16); the *Hay Wain* reproduced by courtesy of the Trustees of the National Gallery, London; photograph of Canterbury Cathedral from the south-west © Woodmansterne; cover photo reproduced by kind permission of Ben Johnson

# Introduction

*The human chain of pioneers of the Modern Movement that extends back from Gropius to William Morris, and beyond him to Ruskin, Pugin and William Blake, does not extend forward from Gropius. The precious vessel of handicraft aesthetics that had been passed from hand to hand, was dropped and broken, and no one has bothered to pick up the pieces.*

PETER REYNER BANHAM, 1960

WHEN Peter Reyner Banham (1922–88) wrote these words he was living at the end of the sixth decade of the twentieth century, and he considered himself to be a man of the Second Machine Age. In the short introduction to his book *Theory and Design in the First Machine Age* he drew a distinction between what he called 'The Industrial Age', something that had lasted for a century and a half, and a 'Second Industrial Age' that he thought was beginning 'with the current revolution in control mechanisms' – undoubtedly a reference to the potential of automated production systems under the direction of computers. Although he nowhere uses the word computer, the Digital Equipment PDP-1, the first commercially available computer based on the transistor, was introduced in 1960, the year that *Theory and Design* was published.

More specifically than 'Industrial Ages' – as the title of his book makes clear – Banham also identified 'Machine Ages'. He gave no precise dates for what he christened 'The First Machine Age', but clearly he believed that it ran from the last decades of the nineteenth century to some point in the 1930s prior to the outbreak of the Second World War. This 'Machine Age' was characterized by the arrival of 'electric power from the mains' (a national grid as opposed to separate sources of electric power generated on the spot), 'and the reduction of machines to human scale' (the introduction of domestic and manually controlled machines such as cars, aeroplanes, vacuum cleaners or typewriters).

Because Banham saw himself as dwelling in a Second Machine Age, he treated the development and use of the machines of the First Machine Age – principally its buildings, but also what he called its own 'symbolic machine' the motor car – as an historical subject. Unlike later authors, he spent little time on precise starting and finishing dates; as he once observed on another occasion, in this field he preferred to deal with 'mosts' rather than 'firsts'.[1] As he saw it, the idea of the First Machine Age evolved from nineteenth-century Arts and Crafts theories about fitness for purpose and new materials, and was overwhelmed by

**1** Peter Reyner Banham (1922–88), author of *Theory and Design in the First Machine Age.*

**2** Richard Buckminster Fuller (1895–1983), photographed three weeks before his death.

the idea of a Second Machine Age only because its guiding assumptions, such as Le Corbusier and Ozenfant's notion of an already-achieved machine evolution towards 'pure types', increasingly failed to fit the still-evolving facts of material culture. In the end, all Banham's artists, architects, designers and theorists of the First Machine Age (with the possible exception of Richard Buckminster Fuller, to whom we shall shortly turn) go down under the juggernaut of continuous technological evolution.

When it came to the Second Machine Age (which was not of course the subject of his book), Banham was no more forthcoming. At one point in *Theory and Design* he characterized it as the stage of technological evolution at which 'highly developed mass production methods have distributed electronic devices and synthetic chemicals broadcast over a large part of society'. At another he suggested that there were no adequate descriptors because 'we lack a body of theory proper to our own Machine Age' and are still 'free-wheeling along with ideas and aesthetics left over from the First'. Although he did not elaborate on the subject in the way that I endeavoured to do 14 years later in my own book *The Private Future*,[2] Banham did touch on and understand the socially atomizing effect of the new Second Machine Age technology. He saw that the railway train and the cinema of the First Machine Age did not change home life or individual human relationships in the drastically fundamental way that the car or television did. But he never wrote a book about human

2

resistance to technological change, or its effect on theory and design – although he did once christen it 'The Wampanoag Effect' – after the name of a technically revolutionary American naval vessel of the nineteenth century.[3]

Because *Theory and Design in the First Machine Age* was intended to be history, not prediction, Banham's introductory remarks about the nature of the Second Machine Age were chiefly concerned to establish a rudimentary platform for looking back on the First. This is important, not only because it legitimizes the interest in the field taken by another author – however differently disposed towards the same subject matter – but because it explains the incomplete nature of Banham's judgement on the interface between the two ages. In so far as we can judge from *Theory and Design*, the key technical separators between the two Machine Ages were the advent of domestic electronics and the massive spread of process control mechanisms. More interesting to Banham in the late 1950s was what he saw as the liberating social impact of these innovations. He thought they had brought about the end of the control of machines by an elite, something that had been a key characteristic, not only of the First Machine Age, but of the century of industrialization that had preceded it. In his way of seeing this change, as in his way of seeing the possibility of social atomization by technology, the Banham of *Theory and Design* was original but undemonstrative. Reyner Banham was essentially an optimistic writer – any collection of his journalism will reveal this characteristic above all others, except his wonderful insight into material culture as a whole – but the downside of optimism is a dogged refusal to dig deep into ominous portents. Reyner Banham stopped where the nightmares of technology began.

Today, nearly 30 years later, the great weakness of theory and design in the Second Machine Age is not so much that it has failed to provide a sequel to Arts and Crafts, as that it has failed to produce any unifying theories at all, such theories being interpreted as 'suppositions explaining something, based on principles independent of the phenomenon to be explained' – as *The Concise Oxford Dictionary* puts it. This failure is remarkable, all the more so in view of the veritable explosion of writing about architecture that has taken place since the collapse of consensus support for Modernism some 15 years ago. Indeed, it is a failure so conspicuous that it might be argued that all the writing, theorizing and televising that has taken place in the interval has had the opposite effect: it has not so much explained architecture as buried its driving force, the social purpose of building, a purpose that in the Modern era generated a model relationship between theory and practice.

The Second Machine Age is an age without ideology, and its books are not theoretical. As in the eighteenth century, at least until the French Revolution, they are more likely to be collections of images with a bland, soothing text laid like wall-to-wall Berber carpet between them. Where 50 years ago, at the height of the Modern rebellion, volumes like *The Modern House* by F. R. S.

3

Yorke, or *Fine Building* by Maxwell Fry[4] contained urgent texts and clear plans urging principle and practice – both authors were themselves architects – their equivalents today would be more likely entitled *Fifty Modern Houses* or *Contemporary Architecture of Alaska*,[5] and the authors would no longer be architects but academics or journalists. Nor of course would there be plans of the buildings illustrated: an increasing number of building owners forbid publishers to reproduce the plans of buildings for security reasons.

This new way of looking at buildings without at the same time considering what they are for or how they are made has supplanted the analytical enlightenment of the Modern era in a way that neither Reyner Banham nor anyone else in 1960 could have expected. It is part of a wilful rejection of the rule of theory that is international, and by no means confined to the producers and purchasers of architectural books. Architects too have learned to become visually instead of ideologically oriented, and the intellectual substance of their discourse has changed accordingly. Today they are not in the sociology business but in the imaging business, just as much as the magazine and book publishers, the TV producers, the art editors, photographers and writers of the media. All of them behave as though the old world of historical time has been telescoped by perfect colour photography into a kind of illustrated catalogue of the built environment. With the stripping away of the real historical context of plan, structure and ideology, all architecture has been reduced to imagery, and all imagery is available to be used in any combination. There can be Mayan shopping centres, Gothic petrol stations and Renaissance electronic banks. Today all the features ever included in any building, from the stone reliefs of the temples of Abu Simbel to the perforated steel sunscreens of the Hongkong and Shanghai Bank, can be mixed and matched and applied to any other building under the name of 'historical references'. The result has been a voluntary abandonment of the old logic and reason, that is paralleled by the decline of democratic authority in a society that is fragmenting, one whose dissembling politics take place much better behind façades that are at best enigmatic and at worst false.

Today architects no longer think it remarkable that replicas of this or that architectural style should be shrink-wrapped over the same multifunctional serviced floorspace, irrespective of period or context. The process is as absurd as the computer wargaming that permits the Emperor Napoleon to fight Robert E. Lee, or Alexander the Great to break through in the Ardennes; but architects, officials and commentators take it seriously enough to argue at length at public inquiries over which spray-on elevation is most appropriate to which historical setting. The architecture that results is exactly like one of the selective evocations of the past that appear in television commercials, with historical veracity achieved by a few bars of Dvořák and sepia-tone streetscape. On TV, as in architecture, this superficiality is enough. It is unnoticed by the historically illiterate, even as it reduces the historically literate to helpless rage. 'It was not like that,' is all they can say finally. But it is like that now, and it will be from now on, for the change in perception that makes real history unimportant is permanent and irreversible. Real history has been 'used up' and, like old movies, it is now fair game for packaging in 'seasons' of this or that director, star, producer – or architectural style.

The conquest of theory by imagery is not a superficial phenomenon. It reflects deep changes in the structure and task of the architectural profession. Stylistic banter may have sunk the once clinically prescriptive language of Modern architecture to the level of banality of the fashion page, but it could not have done this if key areas of real expertise had not already vanished from the architects' grasp. With the vastly increased complexity of almost all building projects, the control of building works – once regarded as crucial to the integrity of architectural ideas – is in the process of disappearing into the hands of a new discipline called project management. Circumscribed 'design consultancy' has become the normal pattern of engagement, and with it the Modern taste for daring innovation, chastened by building failures and massive professional indemnity insurance claims, has been replaced by a conservative desire to avoid risks. Planning officers too have taken upon themselves more and more of the effective decision-making about the content and appearance of building projects. In architectural practice the consequence of disputes with planning and building control officers, in terms of delay alone, can be serious enough to force almost any compromise, and this too has an increasingly inhibiting effect.

As a consequence of the dismantling of professional privileges to facilitate free competition, professional standards too have declined. Architects retain one important power, and that is the power of specification. The architect effectively decides, even if he no longer designs it himself, who is going to receive the £15 million order for the steelwork or the £7 million order for the curtain walling. This role as selector of materials and components is now the core of the status of the architect in the construction industry. It ensures that a steady supply of component and materials advertising is directed towards architects; and that advertising in its turn supports the culture of architecture that is kept alive in books, architectural magazines, newspapers and television programmes. Even if architects have ceased to design buildings from the inside out in the Modern sense, as long as they continue to choose key components and finishes they will remain in effect 'licensed specifiers', with powers and responsibilities similar to those of doctors of medicine who prescribe drugs. As a replacement for the *carrière ouverte aux talents* of their ancient art, this might appear a dismal bureaucratic fate, but it is compatible with what we know of the evolving pattern of construction in the future.

In 1985 the Technology Assessment Board of the United States Congress, the American equivalent to an all-party House of Commons Committee, listened to representations on the future of the construction industry that caused consternation throughout the architectural profession. Harry Mileaf, chairman of the 4,000-member US Co-ordinating Council for Computers in

5

Construction, predicted that four-fifths of the 80,000 practising architects in the United States would be 'dislocated' by the year 2000. 'Construction design is highly labour intensive,' Mileaf explained. 'Producing architectural drawings now accounts for half of all design costs for new buildings. Within 15 years, computer-aided design systems will have automated the drawing process, product specification and cost estimating altogether.'[6]

It is in the context of this evolving climate of competition and obsolescence that we should view the increasing tendency for architects embroiled in controversy over contentious projects on sensitive sites to find themselves sitting targets for unscrupulous competitors. Lured on by the prospect of a kind of 'aesthetic compulsory purchase' by public opinion, other architects prepare so-called alternative schemes. These mischievous commissions are in breach of the old professional code of conduct because their originators plainly intend to supplant a troubled colleague, but the old professional code is on such shaky ground now that it no longer dares put itself to a legal test. In the United States in 1979 a similar anti-supplanting clause was declared against the public interest by a District of Columbia court. In recent years dozens of mischievous commissions of this kind have been drawn up, and often paid for by conservationist organizations. The best-known of these is probably the 1988 John Simpson project for Paternoster Square near Saint Paul's, a commission already in the hands of Arup Associates, but there have been others, notably in connection with the Mies van der Rohe project for Mansion House Square and its James Stirling-designed successor at No. 1, Poultry.

Perhaps the culmination of all these disturbing consequences of the fall of ideology in architecture has been the rise of the idea that there is no longer any need for expert judgement at all where the design of buildings is concerned. 'I know that what I feel in spirit about a building is just as valid a criticism as any professional or technical point of view,' the Prince of Wales wrote to Peter Palumbo at the height of the Battle of Mansion House Square. And in this, as in so many other matters, there is no reason to suppose that his opinion differs greatly from those of his future subjects.

From this Olympian dismissal of the need for an art and science of building design there can be no reprieve. Indeed, for those with eyes to see there is already one visible pattern of destruction that could dissolve the ancient discipline of architecture within the lifetime of the future King. Even as 'architecture' is stretched thinner and thinner over a skeleton of serviced floorspace, the increasingly confident use of the term by the computer industry suggests that it could end up under 'computer' in the dictionaries of the twenty-first century.

Catalogued in this fashion, the dissolution of architecture in the Second Machine Age is a sad story. It is an almost biblical tale of a Fall from Grace, and as such is invariably seen as a warning rather than as a subject for further inquiry. The present critical consensus willingly consigns the period of Modern dominance to the limbo of no longer disputable evils of the past, like slavery or collective farming, subjects that can neither be fashionably advocated nor (yet again) elaborately dismissed.

But convenient as it may be today, this view is untenable in the long term. Less than twenty years ago Modern architecture derived its power from a popular acceptance of its basic principles that was no less overwhelming than the present dismissal of their sad legacy. For nearly 50 years Modern architecture was an idea that drove politics before it and crushed art history beneath the weight of its technological pragmatism. Its arguments for light, air, geometry, planning and industrialization were unanswerable – and even today can be made to appear ridiculous only by denying the need for a policy of continuous development in building – something that is, rightly, still demanded in every other field of technology. In its day, Modern architecture's dynamic thrust into leading-edge technology was no more disputed than is today's delving into space age materiology by the designers of racing yachts and Grand Prix cars.

Why should the architecture of the First Machine Age have collapsed so suddenly? Today the reader searches in vain through the flood of writing of the last 15 years for an adequate explanation of this débâcle. But with the exception of a few paragraphs of cautious uncertainty about whether it really is all over yet, the Fall is always seen as a Deliverance – something that requires no more explanation or justification than the overthrow of a great dictator. 'Modern art and architecture are the perfect expression of the bankrupt faith of a nation that knows not what to do or where to turn,' said Quinlan Terry, the Classical Revivalist, in a television documentary in 1988[7] – as though bankrupt faith and bewilderment were not true descriptors of the state of all humanity in the late twentieth century.

Like the Wall Street crash of 1929 and the stock market panic of October 1987, the fall of Modern architecture was never unequivocally predicted, even by its most implacable opponents. Terry confesses that his mentor, the dogged Classicist, Raymond Erith, who wished for it mightily, did not expect it to happen, even on his deathbed in 1973. The pioneer Modern architect, Maxwell Fry, warned in 1944 that 'if the developments which have led to our present technical skill were to continue at the same pace into this century, at a pace, that is, exceeding our capacity as artists to assimilate them, then our hopes of establishing a workable architecture would be slight.'[8] Apparently a prescient warning, but unfortunately followed by the unjustified reassurance: 'But that is not the case, the main lines of development are now foreshadowed and refinements of pure technique are a simple matter.' In the event only one Modern architectural historian – as opposed to the art historians of the old era who merely opposed it – even began to offer an explanation for the Fall before the event itself engulfed them.

In *Theory and Design in the First Machine Age* Reyner Banham offered a brief obituary for the first generation of Modern architects that was in the nature of a warning of disaster. Despite the brevity of this prediction – it is limited to four speculative pages at the end of a 330-page book – the fact that Banham addressed himself to the possibility of defeat at the height of the global victory of Modernism is what makes *Theory and Design in the First Machine Age* important today.

Consisting in effect of a short critical chapter attached to the end of a long and discursive art history of the heroic phase of Modern architecture, *Theory and Design* as a whole is a text book, not a work of prophecy. What prophecy there is, is second hand, and consists almost exclusively of one long elided quotation from the American inventor Richard Buckminster Fuller (1895–1983), and a subsequent discussion of its meaning. Neither the source nor the date of this quotation (to which we will shortly turn) is given in *Theory and Design*, which is surprising in a volume that is otherwise heavily footnoted. The impression given by the surrounding text is that it is contemporaneous with Fuller's prefabricated Dymaxion House, general arrangement drawings of which were made in 1927 and a mock-up built for the Chicago Exposition of 1934, where it attracted considerable publicity, notably in the business magazine *Fortune*, to which Fuller became an editorial consultant, and which remained loyal to his conception of the factory-built home until the late 1940s.

Surprisingly, none of this publicity was the source of Banham's quotation, nor are either of Fuller's only well-known pre-war writings, an article entitled 'Universal Architecture' that appeared in the Philadelphia-published *Shelter Magazine* in February 1932, and his first book *Nine Chains to the Moon*,[9] which was published in 1938. The quotation is not even from the revised version of *Nine Chains to the Moon* that was republished in 1963. Although Banham nowhere explains this, the definitive criticism of Modern architecture, for which *Theory and Design* is famous, actually comes from a long letter that Buckminster Fuller wrote to John McHale dismissing any suggestion that the teachings of the Bauhaus had had any influence on his work. This letter was dated January 1955.

Unlike the models and mock-ups of the Dymaxion house that Banham uses to illustrate his work, Fuller's letter, which was subsequently published in the magazine *Architectural Design* in 1961, and again in James Meller's collection of Fuller's writings, *The Buckminster Fuller Reader*, in 1970, is virtually contemporaneous with *Theory and Design in the First Machine Age*. Even if the inventor did express similar sentiments before World War Two, perhaps as early as 1927, these words that Banham quotes in *Theory and Design in the First Machine Age*, are not the words that Fuller used then:

The 'International Style' brought to America by the Bauhaus innovators demonstrated fashion-inoculation without the necessity of knowledge of the scientific fundamentals of structural mechanics and chemistry. The 'International Style' 'simplification' then was but superficial. It peeled off yesterday's exterior embellishment and put on instead formalised novelties of quasi-simplicity, permitted by the same hidden structural elements of modern alloys that had permitted the discarded *Beaux-Arts* garmentation . . . The new International Stylist hung 'stark motif walls' of vast super-meticulous brick assemblage, which had no tensile cohesiveness within its own bonds, but was, in fact, locked within hidden steel frames supported by steel *without visible means of support*.

The International Bauhaus never went back of the wall-surface to look at the plumbing . . . In short they only looked at problems of modifications of the surface of end-products, which end-products were inherently sub-functions of a technically obsolete world.

Banham claims of this passage that it is not 'mere wisdom after the fact' because 'as early as 1927' Fuller had advanced in his Dymaxion house project a concept that would have rendered Le Corbusier's Maison Savoie of 1930 'technically obsolete'. He does Fuller no service here. Extracts from a letter written in 1955 that are presented as a statement made 'as early as 1927' are 'after the fact', even if the Dymaxion house project was not. The letter, like Banham himself, belongs to the Second Machine Age, not the first.

Banham does not confine himself to quoting from and citing Fuller. He develops the critique, deducing on the basis of Fuller's 1955 letter that, because of their ignorance of 'the scientific fundamentals of structural mechanics and chemistry', Modern architects 'produced machine age architecture only in the sense that its monuments were built in a machine age, and expressed an attitude to machinery – in the sense that one might stand on French soil and discuss French politics, and still be speaking English.'

Banham's conclusion is:

The architect who proposes to run with technology knows now that he will be in fast company, and that, in order to keep up, he may have to emulate the Futurists and discard his whole cultural load, including the professional garments by which he is recognised as an architect. If, on the other hand, he decides not to do this, he may find that a technological culture has decided to go on without him.

It is clear from the build-up to this passage that in 1960 Banham believed that all building would, in the end, have to conform to the theory of endless development that Fuller had identified and defined as 'ephemeralization' in the 1938 edition of *Nine Chains to the Moon*. Indeed the last quotation from Banham above is very close to being a tidy paraphrase of 'Scientific Dwelling Service', the congested chapter 39 of *Nine Chains to the Moon*, but of course without Fuller's key word 'ephemeralization', which expressed his belief that technology increasingly delivered 'more for less', more performance for less weight and material.

After *Theory and Design* Banham did not return to the crisis point of Modernism, except to present what some might interpret as his own version of the Dymaxion House in the form of the 'Standard of Living Package'[10] designed by himself and François Dallegret in 1965. For the rest of his life he retained his belief that 'what we have hitherto understood as architecture, and what we are beginning to understand of technology may be incompatible disciplines', but in subsequent books he resolutely turned away from the future in favour of history.

With the eclipse of the Modern Movement, Buckminster Fuller too became less interested in the world of architecture and more and more concerned with the evolution of a 'World Design Science' capable of addressing the global problems of population, pollution, starvation and shelter without – as Banham had put it – the impedimenta of the 'cultural load' and 'professional garments' of the architect.

In the 30 years that have passed since Reyner Banham wrote *Theory and Design in the First Machine Age* events have appeared to bear out his prediction of the incompatibility of architecture and technology. With or without regard to the pace at which 'artists' can assimilate it, global product distribution is overwhelming the construction industry, and with it the architectural profession, just as Fuller predicted it would. Today, just as the removal of the badge from the nose or tail of a car can reveal its shared parentage with a different make, so can the peeling away of a decorated façade reveal the homogenization of serviced floorspace beneath the skin of a vast number of apparently disparate buildings. Today's architects have conceded creative hegemony everywhere except in this 'badge engineering' of buildings – the so-called 'signature building' of American architecture – to such an extent that carbon copy engineering – in terms of the names of the consultants responsible as well as the structural and environmental control systems used – is now accepted as the norm. From penetrating deep into the genesis of the building, as it did during the Modern era, the power of the architect over construction has shrunk to the literally superficial: a thin skin on the front of a new building, like the badge on the nose of a car, a small feature on the outside of a refurbished building, a bureaucratic role in the filing of applications and the authorization of payments. An architect's 'capacity as an artist' still offers him this role, but today only the inertia of popular thinking and the politics of the construction industry allow him to escape the modified cry of the small boy: 'The Emperor is as expendable as a light bulb.'

Compared to the great days of Modern architecture, when heads of state begged architects to solve the global housing problem, plan capital cities and design towns, the role of the architect today is tragically diminished. In engineering terms he is hardly a designer at all, his work oscillating uneasily between envelopment by a burgeoning design profession and surrender to the reactionary forces of conservation and historicism. The cruel truth is that, despite their apparent popular success, all post-Modern architectural achievements are isolated from the major technological themes of the Second Machine Age. Failure to keep up with all science, not just material science, was indeed the price that architecture paid for the retention of its 'cultural load' and its 'professional garments'.

In this sense post-Modern architecture can be compared to a kind of impoverished avant-gardism in the cinema, where the same deliberate denial of creative potential for the sake of effect exists. Mainstream cinema exhibits none of its characteristics; no feature film relies on a written programme to explain its action, or adjourns to a live theatre for key sequences, or wastes time with the immobile presentation of solid objects – it encompasses all these phenomena within its power to simulate the restless diversity of human perception. Because architecture has developed no such power of simulation it clings to a narrow vocabulary of antique effects like a deranged film director insisting on a single camera position because the single viewpoint is legitimized by the glorious history of live theatre. From the very beginning all recording and reproductive technologies have diminished the impact and importance of static form.

Today no architecture – not even the revered architecture of the past – can exist without information. All buildings are terminals for information systems, their carcasses are riddled with cables like twentieth-century wood-worm, writhing and squirming beneath their floors, above their ceilings, up and down their service ducts. Compared to the information that is pumped into buildings, whether they be 300-year-old country cottages or born-yesterday air-conditioned science park sheds, any significance they may possess because of their physical form is marginal. And it is this *unimportance* above all other things that has permitted the emergence of a bizarre, homo-genized 'heritage' architecture that is the product of 'licensed specifiers' rather than architects, as history would have recognized them.

According to this new reality, Buckminster Fuller and, by association, Reyner Banham were right – not solely about the First Machine Age but the Second Machine Age too. Architecture is obsolete in 1990, and Maxwell Fry's 'main lines of development' turn out not to have been 'foreshadowed' at all. The result, 30 years after *Theory and Design*, is that architecture has become a slow-moving, inefficient, ornamental target in a video game played by instantaneous information and technological change.

## NOTES

1 'This is less a book about *firsts* than about *mosts*,' Reyner Banham wrote in the introduction to *The Architecture of the Well-tempered Environment* (Architectural Press, 1969). He went on to explain this statement as follows: 'The invention and application of technological devices is not a static and ideal world of intellectual discourse; it is (or has been) impelled forward by the competitive interaction of under-achievers and over-achievers – who might even be one and the same person, for some breakthroughs in application were achieved without matching break-throughs in invention.' This is a prudent warning, and applies with equal force to *Theory and Design in the First Machine Age* (Architectural Press) which was published nine years earlier.

2 Martin Pawley, *The Private Future: Causes and Consequences of Community Collapse in the West* (Thames & Hudson, 1974).

3 'The *Wampanoag* Effect' was the title of an article by Eric Shankleman, that appeared in the *New Scientist* for 22 February 1968 interpreting material from Elting W. Morrison's book *Men, Machines and Modern Times* (MIT Press, 1966). Reyner

Banham subsequently used the *Wampanoag* article – and its theme of an advanced technology ship that was rejected by the U S Navy because it 'would not produce the kind of sailor the American Navy has hitherto reared' – in an essay in Jencks and Baird (eds), *Meaning in Architecture* (Braziller, 1969). Banham mistakenly believed that Morrison had recounted the *Wampanoag* story to prove that the U S Navy was 'culture bound' and reactionary. In fact (see the exchange on p. 102 of *Meaning in Architecture*) Morrison (with whom I discussed this matter at Cornell University in 1973) was a genuine 'conscientious objector' against technological change, in the sense discussed in the last chapter of this book.

4  Early illustrated books of Modern architecture like F. R. S. Yorke's, *The Modern House* (Architectural Press, 1934) and Maxwell Fry's wartime functionalist treatise *Fine Building* (Faber & Faber, 1944) are good examples of this genre. The former was continually revised and went into more than six editions; the latter influenced a later generation, including at least one member of the Archigram Group.

5  These are not intended to be the titles of real books, merely to illustrate a genre.

6  *Engineering News Record*, 22 February 1985, p. 173.

7  'Classicism: The Rejected Alternative', a documentary of the personal views of Quinlan Terry, B B C 2, Sunday 6 November 1988.

8  Fry, *Fine Building*.

9  R. Buckminster Fuller, *Nine Chains to the Moon* (Prentice-Hall, 1938; reprinted, with revisions, by Southern Illinois University Press in 1963, and by Anchor Books, 1971).

10  Reyner Banham, 'A Home is not a House', *Art in America*, April 1965; reprinted in Jencks and Baird (eds), *Meaning in Architecture*, and in Banham, *Design by Choice* (Academy Editions, 1981).

# CHAPTER I

# Four Futures

*An attack upon systematic thought is a treason against civilization . . .*
*Let us remember this when we hear the drumbeat and roll call to return to*
*vernacular tradition.*

BERTHOLD LUBETKIN, 1982

ARCHITECTURE today is like the countryside. Or more correctly, it suffers from the same verbal misuse. For both words are coded terms for an industry, ways of talking about a key element of the economy without accepting its aims or purposes. Thus when commentators and politicians talk about 'the countryside' and what is to be done about it, they really mean the farming industry and what is to be done about that. By using the word 'countryside' they avoid running head-on into the viper's nest of issues surrounding the environmental impact of the industry that produces food. It enables them to discuss an economic matter as though it were a cultural event.

When ordinary people talk about 'architecture' they do the same thing. The use of the word enables them to pontificate about the broad sweep of the built environment without having to become bogged down in the contentious politics, economics and methods of the construction industry – the business that put it all there, demolishes it, rebuilds it and maintains it all the time.

It is the use of magical words like 'countryside' and 'architecture' that make uninformed commentary such a rewarding career in the Second Machine Age. What convincing-sounding people say about architecture or the countryside can be wonderfully outspoken, utterly silly or sublimely wise without the slightest risk of slander or ridicule. This is of course a fine democratic freedom and should be protected, but its consequence, the crowding out of serious discussion of the underlying issues, should be understood as well.

The parallel between 'the countryside' and 'architecture' can be taken further. Both are subject to what farmers call 'the Constable syndrome'.[1] In general people whose lives are not actively bound up with farming make deceptively simple demands upon it. They know what they want it to look like, and that is a famous Constable painting, with cows, horses, chickens, crumbling stone barns and an old mill wheel. They do not want to know anything about modern farms actually being outposts of the chemical industry, with highly trained operatives wearing protective clothing and operating extremely complicated and expensive machines. That does not fit in with their

**3** Constable's *Hay Wain*. The countryside as preferred by the city and suburban classes.

**4** Not the *Hay Wain*. High-tech agriculture with expendable plastic drying tunnels.

image of 'the countryside', it sounds more like 'farming', which has an image that hardly attracts cultural commentators at all.

Building has the same problem. Call it 'architecture', and most people – as the Prince of Wales is no doubt correct in saying – would prefer it to consist of 'curves and arches, courtyards and porches, spires and columns'. But alas, as with the countryside and farming, the popular desire for a universal fairy tale Neueschwanstein is inversely proportional to the people's understanding of the realities of the construction industry. Buildings are the elements of which architecture is made, and for the most part – like the drums of chemicals and propane bird-scarers down on the farm – they have a job to do that, until recently, did not have to be reconciled with the chocolate box image of 'architecture'.

5 Neueschwanstein, 1869. An image as pervasive and illusory as Constable's. Finally (in replica) the centrepiece of Walt Disney's 'Magic Kingdom' in Florida.

6 Not Neueschwanstein or the *Hay Wain*. The I N M O S semiconductor factory in Wales, Richard Rogers, 1962.

It is because the use of the word 'architecture' has become a means of expressing unease about the rapacious consumption of the natural environment by development, that both too much and too little is expected of it today. Even the idea that it is part of the job of buildings to be 'popular' is recent and erroneous. Blaming the physical consequences of the operations of the economy on architects is a childish error which, were it not so wonderfully suited to the concealment of unpalatable realities, would have long since been dismissed as nonsense by intelligent persons. The economy is not an engine for producing images that people either 'like' or 'dislike', any more than a car is a machine for causing accidents. If it were not so sinister, the very childishness of this view would explain the often remarked failure of any architect to make an adequate response to it: they are stunned as much by disbelief as by a guilty conscience.

But childish or not, the trick has succeeded, and today it frames the entire architectural debate. Far from enjoying a public reputation as 'providers' or 'enablers', architects are seen as irresponsible purveyors of harsh reality in a realm that prefers to see its buildings, like its farms, through rose-tinted glasses. 'For far too long architects have consistently ignored the feelings and wishes of the mass of ordinary people in this country,' observed Prince Charles in 1984. 'Architects and planners do not necessarily have the monopoly of knowing best about taste, style and planning . . . ordinary people should not be made to feel guilty or ignorant if their natural preference is for more traditional designs.'[2] How true. But how serviceable such a line of attack can be! It can be turned on farmers (who make food), doctors (who heal the sick), or even the people who burn coal or split atoms to make the electricity without which the expression of opinion (among other things) would be impossible.

In the end the only interesting thing about blaming architects for everything is the certainty that the charge must embody the seeds of a defence. If architects have ruined 'architecture' in the same way as farmers have ruined 'the countryside', by 'spoiling the look of it', then they are front-runners for the job of making it better again by making it 'look all right'. If we so disregard the realities of economic life as to say that 'bad architecture' is the cause of all our present discontents, then we have already committed ourselves to the guaranteed disappointment of a belief that 'good architecture' is the only remedy.

Of course we cannot yet say with certainty what this 'good architecture' will look like, but we already know its name. It will be called 'Charles III' style. In 1988 a newspaper poll[3] showed that 51·2 per cent of the British public thought that the Prince of Wales should vet all major architectural projects – and we have a fair idea what sort of architecture he prefers. Supposing the Prince were to set up an architectural evaluation secretariat at Kensington Palace, we can be sure that its overworked functionaries would be endorsing very few projects that could be compared to 'a Victorian prison', 'an assembly hall for secret policemen', 'a hardened missile silo', 'a municipal fire station', 'a broken 1930s wireless set', 'a carbuncle on the face of a friend', or 'a glass

**7** Plessey semiconductor factory near Plymouth by BDP Architects, 1987. Painted grey after being described as 'a high-tech version of a Victorian prison' by the Prince of Wales.

**8** The 1984 version of Ahrends Burton & Koralek's National Gallery extension, the famous 'carbuncle' and 'fire station with a sort of tower for the bell'. Abandoned after royal attack.

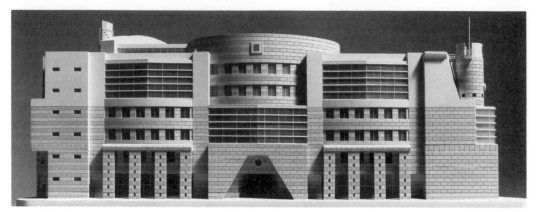

**9** 'A broken 1930s wireless set'. Postmodern project for No. 1, Poultry by James Stirling 1988. Attacked by the Prince of Wales.

stump'.[4] If and when the taste of the Prince of Wales does come to govern the shape of most architecture, then there will undoubtedly be a style called 'Charles III' whose principal characteristic will be that it disguises all machine age operations under a 'Canaletto syndrome' of its own.

Next to its extreme vulnerability to the prejudice of Princes, there is no better indication of the true unpopularity of Modern architecture in the late twentieth century than the extent to which a taste for disguising it has penetrated the building control bureaucracy. Planning, which effectively runs architecture, was founded upon the idea of organized physical control of the impact of development upon the land. Now, like architecture, it has changed. No longer does it base its operations on the enactment of centrally directed economic plans, but upon local development 'opportunities'. Just as the semantic withdrawal from 'farming' to 'countryside' softens and confuses the outlines of rural conflict, so does the effective abandonment of strategic development control in planning create an ill-defined area of political combat where once there was supposed to be a careful expression of national building policy. In London's docklands for example the term 'plan' is no longer used and has been supplanted by the word 'framework'. Nor are such 'frameworks' even drawn up by qualified planners; instead they come under the remit of landscape architects who are deemed to be 'flexible' enough to rub out the green bits and replace them with buildings whenever investment opportunities arise. The entire Royal Docks area was 'replanned' on this basis[5] and there are examples elsewhere. Few could be more apposite than the sudden appearance of plans for 10 million square feet of office floorspace including an 850-foot tower at Canary Wharf on the semi-derelict Isle of Dogs; or the lightning construction of the Gateshead MetroCentre – the largest shopping centre in Europe with 200,000 square metres of covered shopping, parking for 10,000 cars, and its own railway and bus stations – on a site that in 1983 was still zoned as industrial land on the Newcastle district structure plan.

As an indication of the kind of tactical responses that will be made to the strategic arrival of the Channel Tunnel in Kent, and its rail termini in Swanley and Central London, the MetroCentre makes an interesting study. Within two years of its completion, massive weekend traffic jams already made it inaccessible for hours at a time, and desperate efforts were necessary to persuade its thousands of employees not to occupy most of the available shoppers' parking themselves. *Mutatis mutandis* this will be the state of affairs greeting Euro-road and -rail traffic when it first arrives in London. Because the enterprise economy has jettisoned planned public spending on infrastructure, and abolished the metropolitan planning authorities including the Greater London Council, no one is any longer in command of the strategic planning of the city or the approaches to it. In fact virtually all academics in the field of transport planning subscribe to the so-called 'Equilibrium theory' propounded by Dr Martin Mogridge of University College, London. 'If you build a new road,' he was quoted as saying as recently as 1988, 'then people will switch from rail to car to take advantage of it. Very soon the road is as congested as it ever was.'[6] This defeatist talk in the face of global urbanization is typical of the lack of insight applied to the crucial circulation problems of modern cities by those who are presumably paid to try to answer them. Not surprisingly Mogridge found occasion in the same interview to dismiss a £6 billion private sector plan to divert cross-London traffic into a 70-mile network of underground toll tunnels by applying his 'Equilibrium theory'.

The consequence of this state of affairs is that all our cities have become what we might call solid state or postmodern cities – sclerosed permanent entities whose present street patterns and heritage façades are destined to be part of the infrastructure of twenty-first-century life. Through frenzied construction on and over existing road and rail networks and using existing, and crumbling, sewers, it has become as difficult to traverse London on the surface today as it was when it was on fire from end to end during the Blitz. And this is not a temporary state of affairs, according to any reasonable interpretation of the word. Several of the largest current redevelopment projects (which will certainly run late if they are executed at all) are not scheduled to reach completion until late in the 1990s.

The planning structure that exists to deal with all this building today lacks any resemblance to the rigorous prescriptions of the Modern pioneers of planning. Today the 'guidelines' that regulate individual buildings have no connection with the intractable problems of the environment – congestion, pollution and social unrest – which are the true successors to the wartime problems of munitions production and social mobilization that brought planning into existence. What, for example, has the unhistorical notion that all new buildings should 'blend in with their surroundings', or that 'lost' views of Saint Paul's Cathedral should be reinstated, to do with the crises of explosive urbanization, chronic traffic strangulation and polluted air? If the answer is 'nothing', then why are planners concerned with such matters? If the answer is

that planning is not concerned with the macroscopic regulation of the ter-
restrial economy, but only with the regulation of its micro-aesthetics, then
why not dismantle its machinery altogether in the interest of unfettered
economic growth?

The truth is that planning in the postmodern world is an appendage to
development rather than its director. Its apparent concern with aesthetics and
history is a substitute activity. Every opinion has a function and, in planning,
every mobilized opinion has a function that can be valued in thousands if not
millions of pounds. In the creation or denial of development opportunities,
aesthetic argument has the function of 'crowding out' (as the economists say of
other matters) all consideration of substantive macro-environmental issues.
The conservationist preference for 'junk' architecture – classical façades in
towns and cities, and pitched roofs, traditional materials, funny windows and
decorated brickwork elsewhere – serves the obfuscatory purposes of a non-
plan enterprise economy perfectly. Tinkering with such elements in the
planning debate has become a substitute for calling a spade a spade: facing the
fact that business and money lie at the root of development, not the make-
believe gallery of façades consisting of distinctions without differences that the
public is encouraged to talk about.

With the departure of substantive planning, it is into this derisory context
that the approval or disapproval of the design of individual buildings has now
fallen. The elementary principle that all new buildings, even those of an
unhistorically enormous size and volume, should form a stylistic blend with
those surrounding them, is the most powerful idea in planning today. It has
eclipsed all practical consideration of matters relating to function, energy
consumption, environment or cost. Its more libertarian variant, 'giving every
period its chance' is, if anything, even more irresponsible. In practice it means
not only that new buildings blend in, but all styles of architecture, including the
style-less functional modern architecture of the postwar period, should be
treated as of equal value to Early English or Rococo and defended against
improvement or demolition on art historical grounds. The 1987 battle over the
demolition of James Gowan's Schreiber House in Hampstead, and its 1988
successor over the proposed recladding of Erno Goldfinger's 1963 Alexander
Fleming House at the Elephant and Castle are both classic examples. In the first
case not only did a galaxy of conservationists compete to prove their broad-
mindedness by defending an expendable functional building, but in the latter
they actually obstructed the up-rating of a woefully obsolete complex of office

10   OPPOSITE TOP A view from Somerset House, after Canaletto, showing Saint Paul's. An
image difficult, but not impossible, to paste over present-day urban reality.

11   OPPOSITE BOTTOM Not the Canaletto view. A modern photograph taken from a nearby
position.

towers – with certain well-known high-tech architects (who should know better) joining in the suppression of technological advance.[7]

Similarly deadening theories of aesthetic control are embodied in such parroted expressions as 'the preservation of environmental areas' (letting rip with fake heritage design in the spaces between listed buildings); 'conforming to the local vernacular' (insisting on swept-head windows everywhere in the country from Land's End to John o' Groats); and 'treating every case on its merits' (having no policy at all except the line of least resistance to rapacious enterprise). In all these cases what is being talked about is not what is actually being done, and what is being done is quite valueless, even within its own terms of reference. Inevitably all these rules of thumb tend to combine into a form of stylistic proportional representation; a bureaucratized process of design horse-trading where buildings cease to be creative solutions to problems but become compromise deals instead, and architects cease to be anything more than recipients of offers they cannot refuse.

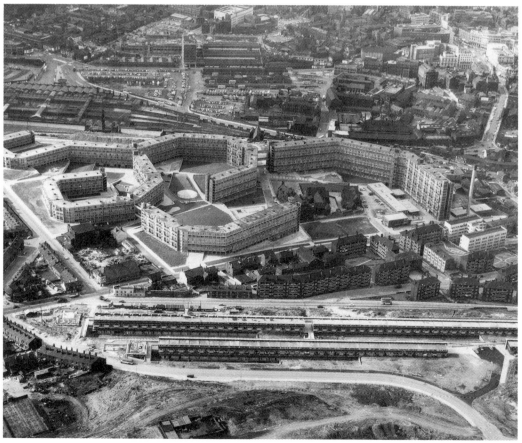

**12** 'Streets in the air' at Park Hill and Hyde Park, Sheffield, in the 1960s. With the aid of hindsight every opportunity a missed opportunity.

It was the defeat of Modern architecture that allowed this state of powerlessness to come about, and the defeat of Modern architecture and its utilitarian complex of theories is inextricably bound up with the history of the two World Wars. In the aftermath of the second war those European cities that were most comprehensively destroyed, like Warsaw or Nuremberg, were painstakingly rebuilt in traditional style; but those that suffered only marginally were torn apart and replanned in the aftermath of the conflict with a resolution and savagery that appears incomprehensible to those who gaze upon the incomplete results today. Between 1945 and 1965 isolated tracts of many British towns and cities were demolished and rebuilt according to Modern ideas, dimmed and fragmented by their journey from a Cartesian continent to an empirical island.

With the advantage of hindsight we can see that every building of consequence erected during that time was a disappointment and a missed opportunity, from the new cathedral at Coventry to the Royal Festival Hall, from the homage to the Unité d'Habitation built by the old LCC Architect's Department at Roehampton to the utopian 'streets in the air' of Park Hill and Hyde Park in Leeds. Every half-completed traffic engineering scheme unintentionally made confusion out of the past and discredited the present.

During the postwar years many thousands of architects were trained as rapidly as possible and sent out to practise their art. The number of architects in practice rose rapidly, from 6,000 to 20,000 in the 20 years from 1945. Planning called for the construction of New Towns, the removal of jobs to parts of the country with no industry and the construction of a vast motorway network to link everywhere to everywhere else. All this work was begun, but ill-synchronized and poorly executed. For decades public sector borrowing and social security cushioned poor management and obsolescence in everything from medicine to ship building. It was upon this scene that the energy crisis and the great inflation of the 1970s descended like a biblical plague.

Before the decade was out there was a revolution. The British people, led by their tribunes in the media, rebelled. But instead of directing their rage against the politicians who had failed to accomplish the 'white-hot technological revolution' for which they had a mandate, the people were persuaded that the real evil was closer to home. Inadequate planning, lack of research and development, poor workmanship, lack of maintenance, broken lifts, leaking roofs, late deliveries, restrictive labour practices: all these combined with a persistent rhetoric of self-praise to create an atmosphere of explosive dissatisfaction with the built environment. By the end of the 1970s thousands had been to the United States for the first time and had seen airports that worked, shopping centres where you could park your car, restaurants where children were welcome. Between them they decided, with suddenness and absolute certainty, that the wretchedness of England by comparison was the fault of architects and, as a result, the members of a profession from whom as much had been expected as was expected of doctors of medicine armed with the new 'miracle' drugs, became more reviled than Nazi war criminals hiding in the Bolivian jungle. A vast political change took place, in which the public sector was robbed of its resources and its infrastructural assets were sold off. The economy shifted from the production of capital goods to the selling and reselling of debt. As a descant to this grand disindustrialization, newspaper editorials poured forth hatred against architects, journalists threatened to kill them, TV documentaries were devoted to lugubrious trips around massive council estates.[8] Architects began to be sued for professional negligence and, for the first time, the cost of insuring themselves against claims became a serious drain on their finances.

The result of this crisis was the disappearance of the hegemony of architectural theory in the built environment. The active Modern perspective of architecture as a tool in the reorganization of society for the collective betterment of man gave way. No longer masters of the universe of the built environment, architects became just another self-serving professional species struggling with the problems of natural selection in the market place. The harsh political and economic climate of the early 1980s, which took away their mandatory fee scale (preventing architects from underbidding one another), and made a dead letter out of their protectionist 'code of professional practice', propelled them from their traditional position behind the arras to an unprecedented orgy of public self-examination. Condemned to the new role of scapegoat, the quickest-witted and most opportunistic of them abandoned the prescriptive mode of the post-war years and humbly sought to learn what the public wanted instead of telling it what it needed. What they learned was that, in the new post-industrial, post-socialized economy, there were four possible futures for architecture.

The first and most important escape route from the wrecked ship of Modernism was to learn to bow to the simple notion of the superiority of the past. This idea was succinctly encapsulated in a leader in *The Times* published some three years before the Prince of Wales's 1984 Hampton Court speech; 'The thing a building most needs to secure public affection is to have been standing a very long time. This is a quality hard to achieve in new construction.'[9] Hard, but not impossible. The rise of a whole popular movement dedicated to the proposition that the only good building is an old one is one of the social phenomena of our time, but it is not as resistant to the possibility of new construction as its leaders might at first have imagined.

Conservation is a vast subject, but here we are concerned only with the supine adaptation of the architectural profession to its demands. This might be said to have begun as late as 1962, when the postwar property boom was riding high and developers were tearing down everything in their path in a ruthless continuation of the wartime destruction that had already anaesthetized the population to the spectacle of piles of rubble in the streets. Antique curiosities like the Coal Exchange had already been destroyed; Euston Station and its triumphal arch were the next Victorian piles destined for the dustbin of history. At this point little groups of well-meaning individuals led by the Society for the Preservation of Ancient Buildings, the National Trust, the Victorian Society and the Georgian Group coalesced. Former supporters of Modern architecture, like the late Sir John Betjeman who had written in 1939 in praise of the 'honest, plain structure of steel, glass and/or concrete' in Soviet Russian buildings, changed sides to support them. The new alliance fought a bitter lobbying battle to save Euston, 'the first metropolitan railway terminus ever built' and, when they lost that, fought again to save the arch and lost again. But it was a pyrrhic victory for the forces of Modern development, at least in London. From then on they steadily lost ground. Major skyscraper projects like New Zealand House were cut down to mere stumps from their original height. The concentric rings of urban motorways that were a key part of Abercrombie's London master plan were scrapped.

Ten years after Euston Arch a 96-day public inquiry into the proposed redevelopment of Covent Garden culminated in the approval of the plan – and the simultaneous listing of 250 old buildings so as to make it impossible to execute. Twenty years after Euston Arch a major commercial development at Vauxhall was stopped dead by the conservationist lobby. With the powerful reinforcement of the Prince of Wales, the same forces next stopped a competition-winning design for the National Gallery, and then the execution of a Mies van der Rohe-designed tower and public square near the Bank of England. Later still a proposed redevelopment of the office buildings north of Saint Paul's Cathedral ground to a halt following the intervention of the Prince of Wales. By the mid-1980s the conservationists had consolidated their power throughout the land. Their watchdog voluntary societies were organized into a seamless network represented at the highest levels of government by a publicly funded umbrella organization called English Heritage. Twenty thousand architects, many of them trained in the 1960s when they were told that their task was to design 'a new, organized surface of the earth',[10] put away their plans and put up no resistance. Taken together, the conservation organizations disposed of hundreds of millions of pounds in commissions for restoration and repair. Besides, there was a new generation of architects coming to maturity prepared to design according to the discipline of Classical architecture as though the Industrial Revolution and the Modern Movement had never happened.

The most famous and most principled of these Classical Revival architects was Quinlan Terry, a disciple of Raymond Erith, an unregenerate Classicist who, at the highpoint of the Modern tide, had been entrusted with such commissions as the refurbishment of No. 10 Downing Street. Terry, as a student in the 1950s, had endured enough ridicule for his dogged espousal of Renaissance design at the AA school to put iron in his soul. He was no expedient convert to Classicism. He believed that Classical architecture was founded on principles that were handed down from God and consequently that

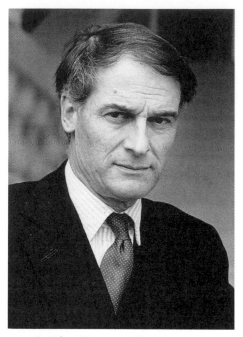 

**13** Quinlan Terry: a Classicist convinced that all Modern art, including architecture, leads to suicide.

**14** Richard Rogers: a Modernist doggedly refusing to oblige.

they could be made to cover all modern eventualities. His work, at first provincial and modest, soon became better known. With the downfall of the Modern Movement he found commercial clients who were more than prepared to have their serviced floorspace dressed in eighteenth-century clothes, provided the resultant designs sped through the planning process without let or hindrance.

Terry's most brilliant success along these lines so far has been his riverside office complex at Richmond completed in 1988. A 150,000-square-foot multi-storey development with an exterior that follows the picturesque tradition in resembling a cluster of grand eighteenth-century houses, internally Richmond is an undistinguished modern office and retail complex fully equipped with modern environmental services and boasting an underground car-park for 100 cars beneath the concrete raft that supports its cobblestones.

Despite its anachronisms, Richmond is a dazzling *tour de force*, apparently an utter opposite to Richard Rogers's high-tech Lloyd's building further down the river. But in fact the compromises at Richmond are equal and opposite too. At Lloyd's the exterior is as uncompromisingly technological as Richmond is Classical, but inside Richmond is merely bare – not meretricious. At Lloyd's, in a perfect example of creative architecture forced to do a deal, the ruthlessly high-tech lower underwriting floors give place to Louis Quatorze-style executive offices higher up the building. And these floors, redecorated at great expense by a French firm of interior designers, are complemented by a

**15, 16, 17, 18**   Richmond Riverside, 1987, and the Lloyd's building, 1986. Two examples of 'creative architecture forced to do a deal'. The contrast between the Georgian exterior of Terry's Richmond (top left) and the bald commercial interior (top right) is stark – but not as stark as the 'almost schizophrenic demarcation' that allows a complete room from an eighteenth-century stately home (bottom left) to be installed above the ruthlessly functional underwriting floors at Lloyd's (bottom right).

complete 1761 Robert Adam room from the stately home of Bowood House installed on the 11th floor. Where Richmond shows compromise, Lloyd's displays a clear, almost schizophrenic demarcation between two irreconcilable approaches to design.

If an initially passive, but soon active, collaboration with the regime of the conservationists was the first future to beckon from beyond Modern architecture, the second involved the development of a new post-Modern style of design. This tendency, which rapidly became a 'movement', was not the outcome of architectural practice. Instead it came to life in the studies and lecture rooms of academic architecture where today's architectural thinkers are obliged to invent movements to advance careers which – no less than those of miners and fishermen – depend on productivity. The more movements they can give names to, the more picture captions they can write, the more successful they will be. But already standards of productivity are high: Sir Banister Fletcher in his famous *History of Architecture*, a monstrous tome first published in 1896 and now in its 18th edition, found 40 different styles from the time of the Pharaohs to the last years of Queen Victoria. The more rigorous architectural historian, Fritz Baumgart, writing 70 years later, detected only 13 styles in the 6,000 years from ancient Mesopotamia. Far more successful was the Anglo-American architectural critic Charles Jencks who, in a 1973 book entitled *Modern Movements in Architecture*, found no less than six styles in the 40 years from the end of the First World War.

The starting date for postmodernism in architecture is characteristically unclear. To me it is clearly foreshadowed in the Classical caryatids supporting the entrance porch of Berthold Lubetkin's otherwise ruthlessly modern 1938 'Highpoint II' flats in North London, but architectural historians do not share this view. Nikolaus Pevsner, writing in 1966, claimed that Sir Denys Lasdun's Royal College of Physicians building in Regent's Park was the first postmodern building. Charles Jencks, the style's most loquacious analyst, claimed in 1977 that postmodernism began with the demolition of part of a notorious Modern St Louis high-rise housing project – Pruitt Igoe – 'on July 15th 1972 at 3.32 p.m.'.[11] Alas, he was later forced to admit that the date was incorrect – or 'symbolic' as he chose to put it.

This uncertainty is characteristic; in some ways it resembles the residual doubts about authenticity that always haunt the world's great paintings. Postmodernism in architecture is no more and no less important than Third Party politics in the British electoral system. The venerable Modernist Berthold Lubetkin (despite his enigmatic caryatids) might dismiss the work of James Stirling, Terry Farrell and Jeremy Dixon as 'Hepplewhite and Chippendale in drag',[12] but at the age of 85 he was no longer currying favour for future commissions – if indeed he ever did. The author has twice witnessed Berthold Lubetkin 'put to the question' on this matter when addressing groups of younger architects. 'But surely if you were in practice now, you would behave as we do and not be as intransigent as you were then?' he is asked. To his credit, Lubetkin never concedes this point, but younger architects with mortgages and overdrafts and less resolution look with a mixture of awe and anxiety upon the achievements of the postmoderns like Ron Sidell and Paul Gibson – who won the Trafalgar Square Grand Buildings competition in 1985 with an exact copy of the Victorian building that was already on the site. What, they wonder gloomily, if they are right?

It is in the twilight zone of the enterprise culture where architecture meets money that the fate of postmodernism will ultimately be decided. Some postmodernists have proved adept at moving through planning minefields to immense commissions, notably Terry Farrell at Alban Gate and Charing Cross, and of course Sidell and Gibson at Grand Buildings; but others like James Stirling in the City of London seem to be unable to satisfy the more discriminating and powerful leaders of the conservation lobby. For these inscrutable persons[13] England as a museum of Georgian buildings interlaced with high-tech science parks is a commodity that is saleable to the £7 billion tourist industry, but England as a collection of cheap architectural jokes is not. The non-specific historicism of postmodern design may go down well enough where even the most erudite critic sees no objection to Corinthian capitals and cyclopean masonry side by side in the same structure – or 'more Venetian windows than there are in the whole of Vicenza', as Philip Johnson proudly boasted of his enormous International Place complex in Boston. But in Britain the greatest enemy of postmodernism in architecture is not the future but the past. In building, as in T V dramatizations, a heritage culture is inclined in the long run to prefer straight copies of the classics to eclectic symbolism.

Classicism and postmodernism are two architectural escape routes from Modernism: a third is 'High-Tech'. The term itself was originally a mid-1970s

**19** Berthold Lubetkin. A Modernist old enough to remember the songs of the Russo–Japanese war. Young enough to dismiss postmodernism as 'Hepplewhite and Chippendale in drag'.

**20** The bridge of HMS *Belfast*, 1938, showing the pattern of exposed servicing that was to be exploited for its aesthetic effect 50 years later.

American descriptor for a style of interior decoration based on the use of wall-painted supergraphics, alloy car wheels as tables, industrial lighting and storage fittings, and other non-domestic items. From there it leaped across the Atlantic to describe the kind of structurally expressive lightweight architecture that had succeeded the heavy steel frame style introduced by Mies van der Rohe, and faithfully copied in Britain by Alison and Peter Smithson. This architecture had originally been called 'modern' too but, in the wake of an increasing use of light, high-strength alloy and composite components, the new term seemed appropriate. Besides, it was not burdened with the semantic legacy of Modern failure.

As opposed to the relative ease with which we can date the importing of the term 'High-Tech', it is difficult to date the transition from Modern to 'high-tech' architecture.[14] A glance at the superstructure of any twentieth-century warship is reminiscent of the clip-on modules of an oil platform, and thus of, say, the roof of Richard Rogers's INMOS building, if not the service towers of Lloyd's itself. In the same way even a modest naval interior, like that of the cruiser HMS *Belfast* (1938), with its bare finishes and exposed servicing, clearly resembles many current 'high-tech' building interiors. But the earliest architect contender is probably Gunnar Asplund, with his lightweight structures for the 1930 Stockholm exhibition, even though these were temporary buildings, like the mast-structures designed by Bertram Goldberg and Gilmer Black in the late 1930s.

**21** Oxford Ice Rink by Nicholas Grimshaw, 1984. An interior reminiscent of a mid-century warship below decks.

Today 'high-tech' architecture occupies a unique status in British architecture. The relative power of patronage of the major sectors of the British economy can be gauged by the fact that in 1987 financial services earned £20 billion in foreign currency, tourism £15 billion, and oil £12 billion. Ten years ago, when North Sea oil first came on stream, the order was reversed. Oil was the national salvation and the image of the battleship rigs and platforms dotted over the bleak sea, their gas flares luridly reflected in the waves, dominated the national consciousness. Inevitably it was at the height of this oleaginous economic rescue operation that the Lloyd's Insurance conglomerate commissioned a new headquarters from Richard Rogers, cast in the shape of a mighty oil rig, clad in stainless steel, moored in the financial centre of the capital city. Oil was king, and offshore engineering gave more than a shot in the arm to high-tech architecture.

**22** Sketch by an anonymous British Petroleum artist showing a North Sea oil platform transposed to the centre of Edinburgh in 1971. An uncanny foreshadowing of Lloyd's.

But as the eighties progressed the oil prices began to fall, and when they did the financial services industry and the tourist industry that had been created out of energy profits began to develop an architectural image of their own. In the world of financial services created by the recycling of Arab oil revenues, the oil rig aesthetic was swiftly overwhelmed by heritage façadism – its labour-intensive buildings, heavily dependent on heat-producing, space-consuming electronic information technology – soon developing their own identity. Vast clear-spanned dealing rooms, their structural slabs separated by up to 5 metres, with raised floors and suspended ceilings packed with air conditioning ducts and cabling between, came to be christened 'New Age' or 'Third Millennium' developments. After Lloyd's the external appearance of these buildings ceased to be dominated by expressed services; indeed three of the most recent buildings conceived for the financial services sector in London, James Stirling's Mansion House Square project, Skidmore Owings and Merrill's later phases of Broadgate, and Terry Farrell's Alban Gate, all boast a heavy application of external *fin de siècle* decoration. This marks the growing influence of the 'heritage values' of the tourist industry and the conservationist lobby.

Brought to a brief but irrelevant flowering by the temporary cruciality of

**23** No greater tribute to the economic reign of oil. Richard Rogers's Lloyd's building, 1986.

offshore engineering, High-Tech now languishes in an ox-bow lake of development. The largest high-tech project of recent years, Norman Foster's £180 million Langham Place BBC Headquarters, was abandoned in 1985, and the largest subsequent Central London scheme to feature outrigged structure since has been a £14 million Sainsbury's superstore by Nick Grimshaw. Today's public taste no longer favours the overtly mechanistic, because it lacks investor readability and, despite the change of name, appears unable to shake off an association with the failures of the utopian public housing of the 1960s. These drawbacks mean that it presently lies friendless and alone, waiting for the logic of Buckminster Fuller's economics of space enclosure to raise its value in the public consciousness again.

The current work of Michael Hopkins exemplifies the present predicament of an architect who took on the ideology of Fuller's more-for-lessing design science revolution and (as he phrases it), 'put it in the bank years ago' – only to

**24** RIGHT Architect Michael Hopkins. High-tech triumph: then compromise.

**25** BELOW Michael Hopkins, architect's own house, London, 1976. Ruthless in steel and glass.

find himself heading a successful practice in a world that no longer recognizes its importance. Hopkins is under no illusions about how backward the construction industry is compared to aerospace or even yacht construction, but he has designed in a high-technology mode ever since he left the Architectural Association nearly 30 years ago. He talks about 'the dreadful in-between world' of contemporary aesthetics and the 'repressive environment' it has created, but he remains conscious that as an individual he has not lacked challenging commissions. For years he worked from his own 'high-tech' open-plan lightweight steel-frame house; now his office is located in the epitome of beached high-tech architecture – an exoskeletal, pressed metal and glass 'Patera' prototype factory unit he originally designed for mass production by an industrial client. Only six Pateras were ever built – and he bought the registered design back himself from his original client.

Appropriately enough Hopkins's best known high-tech job was also for the oil industry; his 1985 Schlumberger petroleum research building in Cambridge was actually built as a research centre for oil exploration. A vast hollow square of Patera-derived office units surrounding a mast-supported translucent atrium of teflon-coated glass fibre which houses a demonstration drilling rig and its ancillary equipment, it is situated on an elevated site only a few minutes' drive from the centre of Cambridge, so that its ambiguous, spidery silhouette can be seen from a great distance to the south and west and its membrane is gloriously illuminated at night. Its canted twin tubular steel masts

**26** Michael Hopkins, Schlumberger laboratories, Cambridge, 1985. Teflon-coated glass fibre takes a bow.

stand out like an early experiment in radio with nothing to indicate the unprecedented three-dimensional precision that was needed to locate the support points for the German-made envelope. In the end two firms of engineers were involved, Anthony Hunt Associates for the buildings, and Arup & Partners for membrane, masts and tension cables.

Resembling nothing so much as a 1912 demountable Zeppelin shed, this building represents the highwater mark of the oil rig aesthetic outside London. Lloyd's may have been more expensive and complicated, but squeezed into its network of medieval streets it is virtually invisible until you stand at its feet. Schlumberger is the most prominent symbol of applied science in Cambridge, one of the very few places in Britain still 'licensed' to belong to the modern world. In any other heritage location it would have been rejected on grounds of inappropriateness.

But the £4 million successor to Schlumberger in Hopkins's office was the 1987 grandstand for Lord's cricket ground in London, and here the nature of the commission itself already shows the impact of changing times. Also a

**27** Michael Hopkins, grandstand at Lord's cricket ground, 1987. Tensile fabric again, but watch those brick arches.

fabric-tensile structure, it was chosen by the Marylebone Cricket Club from submissions by five practices, not because of its advanced technology but because it was the only one that proposed restoring and extending an arcade of 1898 brick arches beneath. This building, in the words of venerable Modern architect John Winter, 'represents the point at which the warring factions of modernism and conservation evaporate in the face of architectural ingenuity'[15] – which is a clever way of describing the beginnings of an escape from the trap that space age technology has become – by way of something like a nineteenth-century clipper ship.

At Lord's Hopkins provided a stratified building that moved upwards from heavy load-bearing brick arches, through a light steel frame with concrete block infill, through a lighter steel box floor, to a gossamer polyester membrane roof of sails topped with a spider's web of tensile masts and spars. It is a measure of the subtlety of the design that the ground level brick arches are not refurbishments but are as newly designed and built as the advanced technology roof that floats above them. Hopkins's scheme places a steel-framed tensile canopy structure above the old grandstand. His high-tech contribution consists of new cantilevered steel frame seating levels roofed in with a mast-suspended PVC-impregnated woven polyester membrane coated with PVDF, but this material science did not impress his clients. What got him the job was his sensitive completion of the row of arches.

'Every job teaches you how to do something, so on the next job that comes along you do it again,' says Hopkins. And the lesson of Lord's was not tensile PVC so much as load-bearing brickwork. In his next project Hopkins stepped off from his Lord's brick arches into a strange new world of genuine Victoriana. Another competition victory, this time an £80 million redevelopment project for Bracken House, the old *Financial Times* offices in the City of London, originally designed in 1953 by Sir Albert Richardson, led Hopkins to turn against what he now calls 'the unacceptable face of high-tech' and concentrate on trying to wring yet more good news out of the Lord's brick arches. In the first Bracken House project that he dubbed 'my campaign against curtain walling', he proposed six floors of unreinforced concrete vaults, Victorian style, behind a load-bearing stone and cast iron façade. The demands of heating, cooling and information technology were all to be met beneath a raised floor, and there were no false ceilings; instead the plain surface of the vaults was used to reflect light from suspended fittings, and the mass of the concrete was used to modulate temperature fluctuations.

This project represented a unique historical counter-attack by 'High-Tech' against historicism: 'What we tried to do was to return to real Victorian construction and make it solve modern commercial problems,' is the way that Hopkins described it.[16] But alas the counter-attack, brilliant as it was, proved to be no more than a losing skirmish. Hopkins's project was aborted before it had even been submitted for planning permission by the 'spot listing' of the old building as a historical monument, and now he has reconceived his state-of-

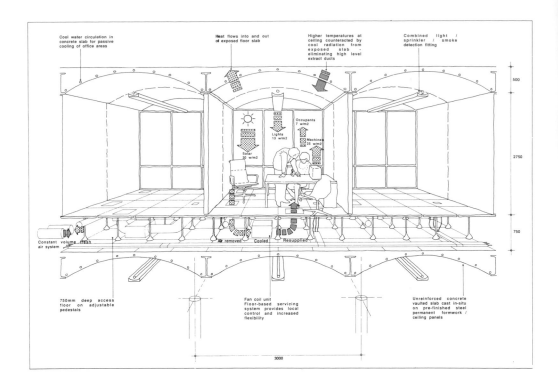

**28** Michael Hopkins, first scheme for the redevelopment of Bracken House, 1988. Daring 'retro' departures with load-bearing brick walls, Victorian jack arches and cast iron structure.

**29** Michael Hopkins, second scheme for Bracken House. Listing of the old building in 1988 brings more 'retro'. New design is 'influenced by Guarino Guarini' (1624–83).

the-art financial services design between the wings bequeathed by Sir Albert Richardson.

Another exponent of 'High-Tech' who survives in a conservation-dominated environment is Eva Jiricna, a Czechoslovakian architect who came to London in 1968 and worked with a number of English practices before forming Jiricna Kerr Associates in 1985. She specializes in interior work and has designed award-winning shop, apartment, restaurant and club interiors for Joseph Ettedgui, Harrods and other clients. Like Michael Hopkins, Eva Jiricna has been successful in recent years but remains pessimistic about the prospects for advanced technology construction because she believes that the cost of tooling-up for new components can never be covered by the return on any single project. Jiricna designed the 3,500 pressed-metal electronic work stations that were installed in the Lloyd's building – but at the insistence of the client their light cantilevered form was masked by teak cladding to make them resemble their Dickensian predecessors. She then lost the interior design contract for the executive areas of the building to the Louis Quatorze-style French decorator Jacques Grange. Today she confesses:

I am resigned to moving very slowly. British clients are very conservative and there is always an enormous time and cost penalty whenever anything involving new materials and methods is proposed. There are no experts in the use of materials like superplastic aluminium, or techniques like laser metal cutting. All the consultants demand massive amounts of information before they will commit themselves and there is no one to supply it but you. Even if you do take on all the extra work involved you still can't increase your fees. I have had to ration myself to a single small technological advance on each job.[17]

Just how small that advance may have to be is clear from the £500,000 design of Legends nightclub that opened in 1987. The most advanced feature is the perforated aluminium staircase with its stressed, woven stainless steel balustrading capable of withstanding more than double the lateral load normally required under the regulations. In a similar but smaller job currently nearing completion Jiricna had to wait one and a half years to get building regulations approval for the removal of a single roof truss and its replacement with a tensile frame because it was deemed 'too advanced'.

Perhaps even more advanced but so far less productive is the 'high-tech' approach of Jan Kaplicky, David Nixon and Amanda Levete who together form a practice called Future Systems. Kaplicky in London and Nixon in Los Angeles have been together since 1979 and have attracted attention chiefly for an advanced technology research project for NASA in the United States, and their numerous competition entries culminating in a much-admired premiated design for the 1989 Paris Bibliothèque Nationale competition. Like Jiricna, Kaplicky is unimpressed with the enterprise of British clients. At the time of writing, the Harrods interior refurbishment he shared with Jiricna is the only major job he has executed in London – although he was a member of the

**30**  Architect Eva Jiricna, daughter of a pioneer Czechoslovakian Modernist. 'I have to ration myself to a single technological advance on each job.'

**31**  Jan Kaplicky and David Nixon of Future Systems. 'The problem with High–Tech is that it is stuck in the Bugatti age and can't even match up to a Ford Sierra.'

winning Richard Rogers Centre Pompidou competition team, and he also worked on the Hongkong and Shanghai Bank and the BBC Langham Hotel project for Norman Foster.

Kaplicky believes that the problem with 'high-tech' architecture today is that, in terms of production, it is stuck in the Bugatti era and cannot advance to that of the Ford Sierra. 'The reason you get better and better products out of the car industry, aerospace and racing yacht design is because they are all businesses that depend on performance to succeed,' he says. 'In architecture success doesn't depend on performance but on value. To get better performance you need a lot of research and development – to get value you only need scarcity.'[18]

Future Systems projects, like the seminal projects of Archigram, lean clearly on technology transplanted from aerospace design, but they reach further into the emulation of organic structures and the inclusion of articulated movement. Recently the deliberate presentation of their advanced structural system projects in the context of conventional architectural competitions has begun to enable them to quantify the benefits of monocoque construction in commercial terms. Like the early buildings of the Modern Movement in relation to their Victorian predecessors, the work of Future Systems cuts through a tangle of unnecessary argument and ornament. Unlike Michael Hopkins, who is trimming his sails to the wind of historicism, or Eva Jiricna, who is in many ways a prisoner of her expertise as a designer of interiors, Future Systems is holding out for the next step in High-Tech – no matter how long it takes.

But it may be a longer haul than any of them thinks. In each of the key cases mentioned so far, Quinlan Terry at Richmond, Richard Rogers at Lloyd's and Michael Hopkins at Bracken House, the want of unity between the interior and the exterior of the contemporary building betrays a conflict between the design values of the architect and the cultural values of the client. At Lloyd's this conflict became so overt that senior managers finally wrested the interior design of the upper floors away from the hands of the architect and his chosen designer in order to restore the semblance of tradition. In the other cases the lesson of the residual value of homage to the past was learned earlier.

While it can be said today that Classical revival, postmodern and 'high-tech' architecture all coexist, there is a fourth form of adaptation to changing economic realities that must be mentioned here, even though it is difficult to identify its real stylistic or economic significance. Community Architecture, forever associated in the public mind with the endorsement of the Prince of Wales, is an example of a heavily publicized minor phenomenon that displaces informed discussion of a major crisis – in this case the cessation of subsidized public housing construction and the selling of council housing that has taken place since 1980.

Effectively the evangelical wing of the home improvement industry, Community Architecture is a movement whose staple diet is the unskilled refurbishment of run-down neighbourhoods. Its essential characteristic is the belief of its members that there is no longer any need for architecture as a specialist discipline. 'The people shall be their own architects,' say its promoters. 'You hold the pencil, we shall design the houses!'[19]

According to community architects, their role differs from that of conventional architects because they are 'enablers' not 'providers'. On duty 24 hours a day (as they claim), they live on site, argue with building control officers, planners and moneylenders, drive dump trucks, lay bricks, and take an equity share in their projects instead of charging fees to clients, who could not pay them anyway. Inevitably their design contribution is marginalized by their belief in the primacy of the wishes of the building owner (or would-be owner) and the limitations imposed by lack of skills and money.

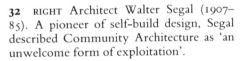

**32** RIGHT Architect Walter Segal (1907–85). A pioneer of self-build design, Segal described Community Architecture as 'an unwelcome form of exploitation'.

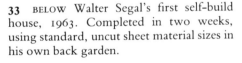

**33** BELOW Walter Segal's first self-build house, 1963. Completed in two weeks, using standard, uncut sheet material sizes in his own back garden.

Interestingly one of the most practical recent contributions to self-build housing, the lightweight timber building system developed by the architect Walter Segal between 1963 and his death in 1985, was expressly excluded by its inventor from the Community Architecture movement. Segal himself was enraged by the 'barefoot architect' concept of 24-hour site supervision, which he described as 'an unwelcome form of exploitation, dragging the solution of the housing problem down to the level of a £40-a-month labourer in the Transkei'.[20] Others have drawn a distinction between those who practise genuine community technical aid, and the entrepreneurs working under the name 'Community Architect' who are in fact developers. And it is true that the best-known Community Architect, former RIBA president Rod Hackney, is better described as a builder and seller of houses who happens to have a professional architectural qualification, rather than as an architect whose principal activity is designing buildings.

**34** Dr Roderick Hackney and HRH Prince Charles on a 1984 visit to Hackney's famous Black Road self-build housing in Macclesfield.

43

**35 (a)** and **(b)** Lea View House, Hackney, 1936 (a) before, and (b) after its refurbishment by Hunt Thompson. The Community Architects recorded a gratifying fall in cigarette consumption amongst tenants.

The only way to measure the real significance of the Community Architecture movement is to compare its contribution to the production (or reproduction through refurbishment) of housing, with the output of new housing achieved by local authority builders after the war. In 1967, the year of highest output, a total of 472,000 new houses was completed in England and Wales – half of them low-cost public sector units for subsidized rent – an achievement unequalled since. So far Community Architecture production figures have never been aggregated for the purpose of comparison in this way, but it is significant that now that the public sector is in the process of dissolution, the 'Community' modernization of 61 dwellings is considered to be important enough to be the subject of a book and more than one TV documentary.[21]

A further irony of the movement is the extreme selectivity of its denunciations of 'top–down' direction in the matter of building design. While Community Architects enthusiastically join in the popular dismissal of the Modern period, with its 'arrogant' social engineering and 'dehumanized' pursuit of leading-edge technology – even going so far as to support the Prince's belief in the expendability of all architectural expertise ('only pedants can argue that the term community architecture implies that the movement is the preserve of architects')[22] – they are by no means averse to making outrageous claims of their own. One firm of 'Community Architects', honoured with the Environmental Award of the 1988 Festival of London for its work on a run-down pre-war Hackney housing estate, responded with a press release claiming that, as a result of their work, 'Vandalism and graffiti are a thing of the past; children have a new found sense of responsibility for their own and each other's property; 72 per cent of tenants now enjoy better health, 70 per cent smoke less and 95 per cent suffer less anxiety and stress.'[23] Compared to this, the propaganda of Modern architecture was commendably restrained.

## NOTES

1  I am indebted for this parallel to my friend James McPetrie who farms 160 acres of land in South Devon. He suggested that 'architecture' and 'countryside' were both words used in this evasive way after seeing the Prince of Wales's 'Visions of Britain' documentary on 28 October 1988. He also used the term 'Constable syndrome' to describe the illusory view of farming possessed by many urban dwellers.

2  From the speech given by HRH Prince Charles on the occasion of the 150th anniversary celebrations of the Royal Institute of British Architects, and the award of the Queen's Royal Gold Medal for Architecture to Charles Correa, Hampton Court, 30 May 1984.

3  As reported in the *Sunday Express* for 30 October 1988. In a telephone survey of 1,000 adult respondents carried out by Telephone Surveys Limited on the preceding day, 51·2 per cent answered yes to the question, 'Should the Prince be appointed to a planning committee to review all major designs?'

4  All these witty comparisons were used by the Prince in connection with various 'major designs' between May 1984 and the end of 1988.

5 Bill Gillespie, senior partner in Gillespies, the large Glasgow firm of landscape architects, in conversation with the author on 6 December 1988, confessed to a feeling of failure about the part his firm had played in 'frameworking' the Royal Docks in this way. Repeated alterations to the 'framework' Gillespies had devised had led to a reinforcement of the barriers between the new commercial developments and the older housing in the area north of the docks, which was the opposite of their 'frameworking' intention.

6 Quoted in Paul Vallely, 'Eating up the Inner City', *The Times*, 8 December 1988.

7 Richard Rogers, for example. In 1980 he said, 'When the Centre Pompidou no longer serves its purpose, I hope they get rid of it' (quoted in Nathan Silver and Jos Boys, eds, *Why is British Architecture so Lousy?* (Newman, 1980)). But in 1988 he supported the defence of Alexander Fleming House against the 'threat' of recladding in aluminium, a performance akin to objecting to the up-grade of a computer system, and quite inappropriate to his beliefs as a high-tech architect.

8 A fairly extreme example was the full-page article in the *Daily Mail* on 28 August 1983 by Andrew Alexander entitled 'Let's Demolish the Planners', which contained the following: 'One day I will murder an architect. There will be nothing personal in it. I shall just check his profession and then gun him down. When charged and tried, my defence will simply be: he was an architect. And I will be acquitted with acclamation.'

9 'The Architecture we Deserve', *The Times*, 27 June 1981.

10 The inspiring phrase used by the megastructuralist architect Yona Friedman at the Folkestone Conference of Experimental Architecture of 1966.

11 Charles Jencks, *The Language of Postmodern Architecture* (Academy Editions, 1977).

12 Berthold Lubetkin, Royal Gold Medal for Architecture acceptance speech, July 1982.

13 Marcus Binney, then chairman of the powerful conservation pressure group 'Save Britain's Heritage', personally intervened in support of the application for planning permission for the Lloyd's Building in 1978.

14 Colin Davies's book *High Tech Architecture* (Thames & Hudson, 1988) is a disappointment in this matter of origins, although the author does have a perhaps premature stab at a termination date with the *Challenger* disaster of 28 January 1986. A veteran classifier like Charles Jencks would never have made such a poor job of providing a starting point for any style he was describing.

15 John Winter, 'Fit for the Test', *The Architects' Journal*, 2 September 1987.

16 All these quotations from Michael Hopkins are taken from conversations with the author during 1987 and 1988.

17 Conversation with Eva Jiricna, November 1987.

18 Conversations with Jan Kaplicky during 1987 and 1988.

19 Jules Lubbock offered this memorable definition at a dinner at the RIBA held on 13 February 1986.

20 In conversation with the author in June 1985.

21 See for instance Alan McDonald, *The Weller Way*, with a foreword by HRH The Prince of Wales (Faber & Faber, 1986); or the videocassettes 'The Pride Factor' (Mirageland, 1985) and 'Community Architecture: The Story of Lea View House, Hackney' (Hunt Thompson Associates, 1985).

22 Nick Wates and Charles Knevitt, *Community Architecture: How People are Creating their own Environment* (Penguin, 1987).

23 Hunt Thompson press release, September 1988.

# CHAPTER 2

# The Lesson of the Motor Car

*There must be a compulsion within mankind to attempt the evolution of objects, as if life itself were being given to them.*

ALEX MOULTON, 1981

TODAY a strong reactionary and anti-technological tendency has been brought to bear upon architecture. Its aims extend beyond the infiltration of the building control bureaucracy and the exercise of power over the appearance of individual buildings, on to the conquest of their very means of conception, the way of thinking that produces their structural skeleton and their internal organization. This is the equal and opposite reaction to the thrust of the Modern era, when revolutionary new forms of construction and internal organization stretched out to dominate the external appearance of buildings and then went on beyond them to visualize the man-made world that Friedman called 'an extended and organized surface of the earth'.[1]

What is the meaning of this reversal? At a time when the preservation of old buildings consumes more attention and resources than the development of new ways to build, the only way to answer such a question is to try to distinguish between the linear, functional development of modern designed objects like ships, cars and aeroplanes – where no such reversal has occurred – and the disturbed pattern of evolution of architectural design. For it is in its apparent developmental incongruence with the general pattern of technological evolution that the central problem of late twentieth-century architecture is to be found. As Giovanni Klaus Koenig claimed in 1988, 'The current Postmodern movement in architecture is going down the wrong road. If the car world, which has greater impact than pure art, and has never been as rational as it is today, has found the true direction, then all industrial design should not hesitate to follow.'[2]

From the earliest writings of Le Corbusier it was a central aim of the pioneers of Modern architecture to wed the ancient craft of building to the newer methodology of engineering, the techniques of mass production, and consequently to the philosophy of ephemeralization, or continuous technical improvement. So vital was the achievement of this polygamous marriage to their way of thinking that their failure to bring it about was a gift to their ideological opponents. As the American critic Peter Blake once observed, 'We can no more imagine the Modern Movement without prefabrication than

47

Christianity without the cross.'[3] And indeed the incongruity of self-conscious architecture, labouring under the weight of a tradition of thousands of years, yet still endeavouring to match the hard functionalism of the shipbuilder and the aeronautical engineer, is an object of gloomy fascination to progressive and reactionary alike.

'The Modern impersonal architecture of so-called functionalism,' wrote Sir Edwin Lutyens in 1931, 'does not seem to me to be replacing the inherited lore of centuries with anything of comparable excellence or to show yet a genuine sense of style – a style rooted in feeling for the right use of materials.'[4] As a general observation made when very few important Modern buildings had yet been built, this was neither inaccurate nor unkind, but it struck at the heart of the Modern failure. Just as accurate and insightful was the observation of the revered 83-year-old Gothic Revival church architect, Sir Ninian Comper, who wrote 16 years later:

The man who sets to work to design an aeroplane or a motor car has no self-conscious strivings to express himself or his age, like the pathetic architects and artists of today. His one business is to make it go and, if possible, to go one better, and he would not be so mad as to think he could do this without knowing the tradition of all that went before. Moreover, if he fails, there is no question of his failure; he cannot hide it by fine words and theories. Let us apply this to architecture and have an end of humbug.[5]

In these two recommendations we have a kernel of apparently conflicting but crucial advice: architecture must master its new materials, yet remain aware of all that has gone before. If its practitioners fail to do both these things they must look to a future of 'humbug'. In fact, 30 years after Comper's death, self-conscious self-expression still rules in those architectural practices where – as a once frequent advertisement enticingly put it – 'Architecture is discussed', and at the heart of contemporary humbug remains the seldom answered question: What really happens when buildings are designed that is so different from what

**36** Still a tantalizingly unmatched image for architecture. The Fiat robot welding line at Mirafiori.

48

comes to pass with cars, aeroplanes, and other complicated assemblages of components?

Today there are people who believe that the design of a building is a cultural event, and others who see it as a business deal. A few perhaps still believe that an act of creation takes place – not just a technical process. Others see an example of management in action, or an entry in a ledger. It is easy to say that the practice of architecture is all these things and more, but evasive too. Just as it is futile to debate world hunger as a moral issue if it is really a technical problem, so it is futile to pretend that architecture is an artistic adventure if it is not.

If the precise category into which the event of designing buildings falls is doubtful, how much more so is its existential reality? Certainly Lutyens and probably Comper had more power over their buildings – and indeed designed more buildings – than practitioners born a century after them. Their world was different. 'It might almost be said of architectural criticism in England in the 1930s that there was none,' wrote Sir James Richards in 1960, 'none at least in the sense of regular appraisals of new buildings . . . Only architects were thought to be qualified to act as critics, and most architects were inhibited by the professional man's reluctance to infringe etiquette by criticising his fellows.'[6]

Nowadays buildings are regularly appraised upon completion. They are discussed as though they were the work of a single artist, who might recognize only the judgement of his peers, and they are discussed as though they were the achievement of a team of systems engineers, who can be judged by anybody because the only thing that matters is whether they achieved a specified performance. Sometimes they are attributed to the patrons who brought them about, or even to the builders who erected them. New cars too are regularly appraised – and generally in a far more objective fashion – but their design too can be promoted either as the achievement of a brilliant stylist, as the product of yet another team of systems engineers working to a specification, or as the

**37** *'Je ferai des maisons comme on fait des voitures'* – well, almost. Prefabricated air-freighted toilet modules being installed in the Hongkong and Shanghai Bank, Norman Foster, 1986.

49

work of the chairman or president of the company. The impossibility of rejecting any of these interpretations out of hand – since in every case there is a measure of truth involved – is an indication of the complexity of the issue. Buildings, cars and aeroplanes can be construed as works of art, as machines, as marketing ploys, or as 'engineering products which can profitably be considered as interrelated functioning bodies connected by sub-systems which in the end largely determine their overall layout' – which is Eder and Gosling's standard definition of mechanical systems engineering, the discipline that produced the Docklands Light Railway and the Space Shuttle. Like architecture, the act of design itself claims multivalency. It can be lauded as a creative act, dismissed as superficial styling, or seen as something to be 'managed' as part of a non-creative team process devoted to 'solving the problems of compatibility that result when many parts are assembled together to form a whole'.[7]

If all the above definitions are true, then the true identity and value of the act of design retreats into the sort of ambiguity that clouds the moment of conception. All a critic can ask is: 'When and in what circumstances is the design of the object, the crucial element in its coming to life?' – as opposed to the bank loan that financed it, or the planning loophole that made it viable, or even the new material without which it could not have been made to stand up. Design always exists somewhere in the subjective relationship between the individual and his or her environment – a relationship that is made real only by the act of creating or changing it. But design can only be more crucial than the act of fabrication – or finding the money to pay for it all – when it is perceived as *the definitive event* in the chain of command that connects needs to resources by way of a new object.

Physiologically any individual, like any organization, assumes a configuration in anticipation of the aim to be served. The individual or the team assumes a 'shape', a shape for doing work, a shape for fighting, a shape for feeling, even a shape for designing. In some kinds of corporate physiology this 'shape' makes the designer prominent. It is this physiology that is present in some architects' offices and not others. It separates the so-called 'commercial' office from the 'design' office. Probably architects have been able to present a distinct identity for thousands of years only because, consciously or subconsciously, as an organism they have protected this 'shape for designing' against innumerable political and commercial pressures.

If such a physiological posturing to protect design does exist, then it is clearly a survival function. But at the same time it may also be the source of all the anomalies that separate contemporary product design from architecture. Perhaps it is because the design-favouring 'shape' of architecture has for centuries yielded individuals 'the pleasure felt from observed modifications on the external world produced by the will of the observer',[8] that it will not undergo the forced marriage with industry and ephemeralization that Koenig recommends.

'The tradition of all that went before' – rightly regarded by Comper as of crucial importance – has protected the creative kernel of architecture for centuries. Art history, the conventional discipline for the discussion of the architecture of the past, is itself a defensive language, designed not to breach this protective posture by demystifying it. For this exotic language of scholarship to give place to the vocabulary of *Mechanix Illustrated* or *Byte*, part of the evolutionarily-learned behaviour of the profession would have to change too; and if that happened who is to say that all architecture would not be lost?

Today it is hardly ever disputed that the proper mode of discussion of the cycle of stylistic revivals of the nineteenth century is through art-historical categories or 'styles'. Greek Revival, Egyptian Revival, Gothic Revival, Romanesque Revival, Renaissance Revival, Second Empire Style, Jeffersonian – all these identifiable types are seen not as existential adventures in the careers of individual heroes; nor as a succession of experimental species of building, nor even as the product of new materials and methods – but simply as exercises in 'style' without existential or technological significance. This view has been defended by, among others, Norberg-Schultz, who claims that 'style has a stabilizing purpose in society because it unites individual products and makes them appear as part of a meaningful whole [that] secures cultural continuity'.[9] That this view is advanced despite the fact that most if not all 'styles' originate as imported innovations and are thus by definition 'destabilizing' is a strong indicator that it is erroneous, but it is in any case of limited significance. More important here is the need to prevent the Modern Movement from being sealed up in this same stylistic tomb before an alternative explanation for its existence can be put forward. Fortunately, unless it is fatally weakened by another half century of anodyne interpretation at the hands of the 'necrophilous disturbers of the graveyards of the past who might at any moment disinter a corpse whose style was still capable of infecting the living',[10] the architecture of the First Machine Age can remain stubbornly outside the laws of art history.

Compared to, say, Greek Revival – whether in its Regency or Edwardian manifestation – Modern architecture was a vast upheaval. It resembled an evolutionary change rather than a minor aesthetic event. So grand indeed were its tremors that they can better be compared to the rise and fall of the dinosaurs, than to any possible stylistic extrapolation of the exciting minutiae that distinguish the shapes of columns or windows. To understand the difference between Modern architecture and say, Greek or Gothic Revival, we must accept that it is a phenomenon of a different order, one less related to the design of buildings than to the evolutionary survival of the species 'architect' in the world.

Like all evolutionary transformations, this one resulted from a drastic change in the environment. Just as the Great Fire of London in 1666 put an end to timber construction in the city and gave birth to brick architecture, and the great Chicago fire of 1871 led to the invention of the skyscraper, so did the destruction of two interconnected World Wars create Modern architecture. To

**38**  Buildings in a hostile environment. Stuttgart in 1945 after Allied bombings.

a lesser extent in 1914–18, and to a greater extent in 1939–45, buildings entered a hostile environment, and the result was that construction all over the developed world was revolutionized. The interaction of the two wars (recovery from one and preparation for the next, followed by recovery from the second) makes it possible to regard them as one: a vast trauma of some 40 to 50 years without precedent in modern times. This was the period that brought about Modern architecture by way of radical changes in the 'genetic frequency' of several building types. These in turn were the cause of massive changes in the 'genetic frequency' of certain approaches to design. Just as a natural cataclysm like an ice age changes the species population of affected and unaffected areas, so did the great upheaval change all building forever.

During the course of the wars themselves many hundreds of thousands of buildings were destroyed; maintenance and new construction ceased, and material and manpower shortages persisted until long after each of the conflicts was over. In Europe and Asia the direct effect of these wars upon the built environment lasted for at least half a century, in some ways it still persists. As a direct consequence of bombing, land warfare and neglect, massive postwar building programmes were undertaken in housing, schools, hospitals and factories. During this period of accelerated construction revolutionary new designs, building materials and techniques which minimized material and manpower input gained within a few years a prominence that they would not otherwise have attained in a century. The old physiological 'shape' of architecture was bent to social and political ends during this period: it was made to make the desperate culturally acceptable. In a later parlance, Modern architecture provided a 'legend' for this transformation.

This was truly a moment of evolutionary crisis. 'The tradition of all that went before' was jettisoned in all save its practically useless art-historical outlines. Experience of traditional materials and methods could not coexist with experiments with new ones. In an unprecedented rupture, the wisdom of the old building trades was thrown away, and the profession of architecture tried to re-educate itself from the scientific laboratory. Nothing like it had ever happened before.

The phrase 'the rise of Modern architecture' is a term that embodies the notion of the abandonment of old ways in favour of new ones. Its implication of new knowledge, if not perfect wisdom, is appropriate, for at first this architecture of innovation, which had been presaged by what we might term 'isolated genetic experiments' before the Great War, shared the undisputed superiority of 'modern medicine' or even 'modern science'. In the crucial conceptual decade of the 1940s it was accepted in the utilitarian spirit of other wartime measures like rationing, mass production and centralized planning.

Thus Modern architecture gained its first firm foothold in an environment of catastrophe, flaunting its new powers as the silver lining of the thunder clouds of war. 'After total war can come total living,' ran the title of a pamphlet produced in 1942 by Revere Copper and Brass Incorporated in the United States. In another called 'Preview of New Way of Life', cast in the form of 'a teleprinter letter' written on 7 December 1946 (not a bad guess for the duration of the war), ex-GI 'Bob' reminds his pal 'Joe' how, when they were fighting, 'We used to wonder if the folks back home were planning anything better to come back to than the life we had lived.' In fact 'the folks back home' have worked miracles. 'Bob' goes on to describe his 1946 house with its retractable louvre roof, solar heating, water supply by condenser and 'radiothermic' cooking. When 'Bob' goes on holiday to Alaska he even boasts that he 'packs up the house and stows it in one of the gliders behind the plane'.

Nor is this revolution confined to housing. 'Total living is more than a fine phrase,' writes architect Lawrence Perkins in another Revere pamphlet. 'It is a

53

**39** 'After total war can come total living.' American Revere Copper Company pamphlets of 1942.

stupendous concept of groups, neighbourhoods, communities and an entire nation more closely knit than ever before.' Perkins goes on to detail new building materials: 'non-ferrous metals and fabulous plastics', and prefabricated house designer Walter Dorwin Teague explains how they will be used: 'We have only to apply to building the same techniques of design, manufacture and selling that have given us a motor car for every four people in the land. In this way the American genius of mass production that is winning the war can win the peace as well.'[11]

The power and force of the vision evoked in the Revere pamphlets of 1942 carried the Modern Movement forward for a quarter of a century after 1945. At the end of that time the house that 'Bob' so enthusiastically described – perhaps with the exception of the louvre roof and the glider trip to Alaska – was a universal commodity. But it no longer looked like the Wrightian Usonian home or the Breuer weekend house or the Neutra sub-tropical paradise that Perkins or Teague had in mind. It had already begun to assume a form that was more and more heavily modified by 'aesthetic' selling features, by the return of the physiological 'shape' of the old design-protective architecture.

Only at the very first pre-war 'genetic experiment' stage, and at this last 'aesthetic' stage was any conflict discernible between the visible process of innovation that was Modernism, and the received ideas about the appearance of buildings that were held by the majority. For a quarter of a century before the date of 'Bob's letter', Modern architecture had battled against a gradually weakening prejudice in favour of ornament and tradition. From 'Bob's' fantasy to the beginning of the 'aesthetic' stage (c. 1970) belief in Modernism as 'total living' – and in its purifying origins in 'total war' – was complete and undisputed. The present ambiguous state of confusion and conflict only grew and worsened later, as the ancient culture of architecture, so deeply hostile to the 'genius of mass production', re-emerged and steadily gathered strength. At this point Modern architecture, having exerted a powerful grip on the imagination of two generations, lost its hold. The environment forced a change again, and it began to merge, like some self-camouflaging species of lepidopter, into the background of history.

By art-historical standards we can truly say that the life of Modern architecture was short: but as an evolutionary phenomenon we can equally truthfully say that it never died. Like a well-trained soldier – which in a sense it was – Modern architecture saw that it was confronting an overwhelming force, jettisoned its strident ideology and its solid geometrical plumage, and vanished into the undergrowth of style.

Could things have turned out otherwise? Because the defeat of Modern architecture in its undisguised form was so complete and so unexpected, the answer must be no. Could things have turned out better? Here the answer must be yes. But in either case, arguing for alternative futures calls for analogies that fit the case with the tantalizing incompleteness of the shapes of continents subjected to the theory of continental drift.

Like its close relative the aeroplane, the species 'motor car' was virtually coincident with the first experiments in Modern architecture. From the beginning of this century the example of the abundant success of its reproductive system was everywhere cited by Modern architects as a model to be emulated. Banham himself describes it as the cause of a 'psychological revolution' because of the power it gave to the ordinary individual; 'Man Multiplied by the Motor', in Marinetti's phrase.[12]

From the very beginning car designers got everything right that building designers got wrong. Car production rapidly reached critical mass. Five thousand small car producers flowered, then withered or coalesced until only a handful of mighty corporations were left. As Koenig has said in so many words, the car designer's product globalized and ephemeralized at precisely the moment when the grip of Modern architecture faltered.

In design terms both species, car and building, went through the same adventures in the last 100 years and both did extraordinarily well out of both World Wars – but there the similarity ceases, for their successes and failures were differently ordered. The history of the motor car demonstrates all the styles and phases of architecture over the last 100 years, but in a way that is not

**40** Mocked-up 'high-tech' Ford Capri with external plumbing shows the drawbacks of the 'inside out' 1986 Lloyd's building.

synchronized with architectural events. In the early experiments of Daimler and Benz we see something like the pioneer work of Wright and Loos. With the Model 'T' Ford we leap straight to the mechanical expressionist or high-tech phase – roughly equivalent to the work of Norman Foster (consider his uniquely relevant 1983 Renault Distribution Centre at Swindon), Richard Rogers or Frank Gehry today. The 1930s sees the automobile designer learning the correct lessons from metal monocoque construction and streamlining in the aircraft industry, with the motor car achieving a classic Modern perfection by 1937 – in the shape of Battisto Falchetto's Lancia Aprilia[13] even more than Ferdinand Porsche's famous Volkswagen Beetle. The architectural equivalent is also a classic of Modern perfection in the form of Le Corbusier's 1931 Pavillon Suisse or Frank Lloyd Wright's 1936 Falling Water – both of which display the same mastery of a new material, reinforced concrete. Then comes the second phase of 'total war', which has precisely the opposite effect upon the automobile to that which it has upon the building. The late 1940s and the 1950s mark the total hegemony of Modernism in architecture, with innumerable rational steel, glass and concrete buildings. But the same decades show a distressing progress towards a kind of premature postmodernism in the design of automobiles. In architecture there is the predictive triumph of *assembly* in the form of Mies van der Rohe's Farnsworth House and the C L A S P system-built schools[14] – predictive, that is, of a rational and economical use of standard

**41** Lloyd's building. Clear space inside achieved at the price of massive surface area and the aerodynamics of a Christmas tree.

industrial components – but with the motor car we descend into the black pit of postwar giantism, culminating in the finned American monsters of 1959. From this swamp of styling the motor car is saved only by the energy crisis of 1974, its design thereafter re-acceding to an enhanced 1937 utilitarian perfection with Giorgio Giugiaro's Volkswagen Golf or the anonymous Honda Accord, perhaps design equivalents in their way to the light high-tech commercial buildings of Nick Grimshaw or Roger Perrin, but certainly as remote from the mainstream of postmodern architectural thought as it is possible to get.

By the late 1980s, after 100 years of development, the Modern, short-life car is as ubiquitous as the Ancient long-life building: the difference is that only one of them still appears in its own clothes. As fast as a land speed record car of 30 years ago, and stuffed with as much electronic gadgetry as a securities

**42** The Lancia Aprilia pillarless saloon of 1937. 'A classic Modern perfection' in its smooth space-enclosing envelope.

**43** Norman Foster's Sainsbury Centre, 1977. Uncluttered interior and smooth space-enclosing envelope both achieved by 'thick wall' servicing. As good as a Lancia built forty years earlier.

dealing room, today's car stands on the brink of another evolutionary leap, into the world of information technology. The genetic frequency of the car, the mobile accommodation unit, which overtook that of all buildings, or static accommodation units, early in this century, is now subject to the powerful multiplier effect of information. Together the mobility and the information capacity of the car threaten the total obsolescence of architecture. Better designed than most buildings – when did you last drive a car that leaked, or see a house with electric windows? – today's car is designed to be built by robots using the minimum materials for the maximum performance in the shortest possible time. Poised to supplant the office, let alone the drawing office, lavish, luxurious, fast, complicated, it bestrides the world of products like Tyrannosaurus Rex. Indeed, the only concern about its future is that it may have literally become a species of dinosaur, insupportable by its own environment, literally running out of space as well as fuel at the apogee of its own development.

For the first time ever the motor car today is facing the kind of attack that revolutionized architecture during the 50 years of Modernism. The environment has turned against it at last – just when its magical success as a piece of industrial design makes the most advanced technology building in the world look like something off the 1913 Ford production line.

Today, at the height of the Second Machine Age, the motor car stands as the best example of continuous product evolution in the history of technology. It has come farther in one hundred years than the building has in one thousand, if not ten thousand. Undisguised by ornament or tradition, it has cut through the forces of reaction that forced Modern architecture underground. How did it achieve this miracle?

Karl Benz's first car of 1885 incorporated most of the basic elements of a modern car: it was driven by petrol, had a water-cooled internal combustion engine with electric ignition, a steering wheel that worked by rack and pinion, and a differential gear between the engine and the driving wheels. The difference between this vehicle and a modern car was that these elements were arranged in an unusual order, and some quite minor ones were given what appears to us to be a disproportionate importance. On Benz's car there were only three wheels; the engine lay flat beneath the seat; the drive was taken off the camshaft and not the crankshaft; the clutch was operated by means of something that could be said to have evolved into a fan belt; the petrol tank was exposed; and the flywheel – an immense circle as big as a roadwheel – was also the hand starting device.

Karl Benz's car evolved out of the nineteenth-century workshop technique for driving machines by means of stationary gas engines, using shafts and belts running on pulleys. Some of these installations survive to this day. Nonetheless to reconstruct the path that leads from Benz's mobile adaptation of them to the modern car would involve patiently researching an amazingly convoluted process of industrial natural selection that removes redundant parts, rearranges and improves existing parts and adds new parts – all in the interest of an unremitting demand for improved performance. The whole story of the car casts this quest for performance in the role of natural selection, so that today's state-of-the-art motor vehicle always represents the survival of the fittest under the rules laid down by its real environment – the legal, technical, financial and physical constraints governing its production and use.

One of the most remarkable things about the interaction between species and environment is that, in automobile technology as well as the natural world, it is irreversible. If no trace of the Benz vehicle remained – but for scientific reasons it was thought desirable to reconstruct its appearance from the evidence of a modern car – the task would be almost impossible. It would require an experiment in genetic engineering as dubious in its outcome as the one by which hens' teeth, which became extinct 6,000 years ago, have been induced by scientists to sprout again – but in the eye of a mouse.[15] In practice, far from working back from today's semi-monocoque 16-valve hatchback to Benz's original, it would be far easier to recreate the pre-automobilist technology of the nineteenth-century workshop and work forward again. This very practical difficulty is an important distinction between the design of cars and buildings, for in the case of the latter the life of the product is so long that the 'missing link' can almost always be found, so that ancient modes of construction constantly beckon from the past.

Karl Benz himself did not take an evolutionary view of the development of the motor car. Apart from the feat of originating it, he played little or no part in its subsequent development. It was always with the greatest reluctance that he was induced to alter any feature of his original design, even when it had clearly become inferior to better-engineered competitors. In the 15 years between its first run and the complete redesign of the car in 1901 – an event which marked the end of direct control of what we would now call design policy by Benz himself – the only innovations were the change from three wheels to four in 1890 and the introduction of a gearbox in 1899. Otherwise the machine remained unaltered throughout its life. It was Benz's belief that, once reliable operation had been achieved, no further development was necessary or desirable. This was a practical and not an aesthetic judgement. Until 1903, Benz cars took no part in motor sport: they were never intended to develop into anything other than a mechanical replacement for a pony and trap. Horse-drawn transportation was the environment that gave them birth.[16]

Unlike Karl Benz, Gottfried Daimler, the only other real contender for the title of inventor of the motor car, did think in evolutionary terms. This Stuttgart engineer ran the first ever motor cycle powered by an internal combustion engine in the same year as Benz drove his *Selbstbeweglicherwagen* upon the streets of Mannheim. Like the latter vehicle, Daimler's first car of 1886 was intended as replacement for the horse-drawn carriage, but its design betrayed an entirely different approach. For a start, it was not a painstaking adaptation of stationary engine technology to the problems of mobility;

**44** Karl Benz's car of 1885 included most of the basic elements of the modern car, but assembled in an unusual order.

instead it was simply a light, four-wheeled horse-drawn carriage with the shafts removed and a Daimler engine installed as a kind of 'power egg' that fitted underneath and drove the rear wheels. The steering gear did not even employ king pins to allow for a tighter radius on the nearside wheel in a turn. Instead the whole front axle rotated around a central pivot, exactly as on a horse-drawn vehicle or a railway train.

The reason for this apparent design weakness was Daimler's belief that once the advantages of internal combustion engine power were realized, all existing horse-drawn vehicles would be converted into horseless carriages. His car was in effect a 'conversion kit', repeating in one move the laborious process whereby horse-drawn coaches had evolved into railway carriages 50 years before. In the event this conversion process never took place; it was a miscalculation on Daimler's part to imagine that it would, and one that throws doubt on his understanding of the limitations of his own early internal

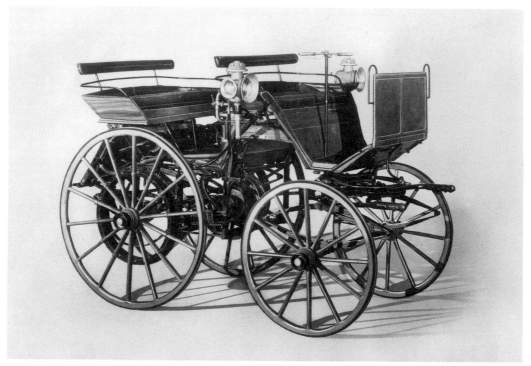

**45**   Gottfried Daimler's first car of 1886 was literally a horseless carriage with a 'power egg' tucked underneath.

combustion engines. But the subtlety of imagination that allowed him to tailor his design so that it could have, was to surface again during the 15 years of rapid development that followed. Where Benz's car gradually declined in status from miracle to laughing stock, Daimler's vehicles progressively shed their 'horse-less carriage' features and metamorphosed into recognizable modern cars.

Daimler's second four-wheeled car of 1889 was a tremendous leap forward. It was equipped with front-wheel steering based on twin cycle forks joined by a drag link, and a four-speed gearbox driving directly on to the back axle. It also incorporated other ingenious features, such as the use of its tubular steel chassis as a cooling radiator for its single-cylinder engine. At the same time its designer was actively pursuing other markets for his engines. He produced motor boats, tram cars, the first lorry, the first fire engine, even engines for dirigibles.

Significantly (in the context of the contemporary rejection of overt Modernism in architecture) Daimler countered the fear of explosion that was commonly associated with internal combustion engines at that time by various disguises. Just as his first car allayed the fears of the technophobes by looking exactly like a carriage without a horse, so did his earliest motor boat promi-nently feature wires and insulators to give the impression that it was powered by electricity.[17] Despite their retrograde appearance neither of these disguises prevented Daimler from innovating in engine and vehicle design. By the time

**46** The 1901 Mercedes, the first Modern car with its elements in the right order. It was the evolutionary destination of both Daimler and Benz.

of his death in 1900 he and his technical director, Wilhelm Maybach, were producing the most advanced motor vehicles in the world. The 1901 Daimler car, called for the first time Mercedes, was triumphant in motor racing and almost entirely recognizable as a modern vehicle. With its four forward-facing seats, pneumatic tyres, mudguards, hood, enclosed engine and side body-work, pressed steel chassis, front-mounted honeycomb radiator and – rare at the time – variable-speed four-cylinder engine, it was as remote from the contemporary Benz as was the Spitfire from a Sopwith Camel.

The design evolution of buildings in the First Machine Age and the Second Machine Age can be looked at in exactly the same way as that of early motor cars, but this is seldom done, even though today, as we have suggested, the use of historical disguise as a mask for technological innovation is particularly common. Not all of the most advanced building technology of our time is obliged to see the light of day first in engineering structures such as oil rigs, aeroplanes and ships. Quite a lot appears behind New Georgian façades every bit as meretricious as Daimler's fake wire and insulators.

The Classical Revival architect Robert Adam, one of the few non-art-historical thinkers in contemporary architecture, has produced his own analysis of this process of disguise and dissimulation. In a paper read to the Royal Institute of British Architects in January 1988, Adam set forth a theory of

**47** Car mocked up for a 1974 advertisement. A perfect analogy for postmodern architecture, as figures 9 and 108(a) will confirm.

**48** Robert Adam's Amdahl Computer Headquarters near Winchester, 1987. Adding Georgian grandeur to a very young and very nervy industry.

**9** Nectar Homes timber geodesic house of 1985, designed by Robshaw Richmond Architects. A grisly result of the integration of 'traditional' elements.

'skeuomorphism' to explain the subliminal insertion of advanced technology into the apparently antique environment of the private housing market and, by extension, into postmodern architecture itself.

Using a cutaway drawing of a typical English 1980s pitched-roof estate house of traditional appearance as an illustration, Adam demonstrated that every material used in its construction was actually man-made or coated, treated, cut, designed, stressed or pressed on space age production machinery. Only the appearance of the house was traditional – everything else, from its chipboard floors to its computer-designed trussed rafters, was already high-tech. Housebuilding today was not reactionary, he said, it was continuously being modernized and synthesized behind a traditional façade. If there are better ways to build a house, the reason they have not superseded the *look* of the traditional house is the entirely practical one that a huge investment in planning, production, trained manpower and distribution would have to be abandoned first. Adam believes that high-tech architects are really calling for just such a massive junking of investment at all levels when they talk about expendable, production line buildings. Because their designs can offer no

**50** An example of Barratt's 1985 'Premier Range' – the type of house purchased by Denis and Margaret Thatcher – it also disguises an advanced construction process.

benefits of the same order of magnitude, he says, they will never get what they want.[18]

But presenting a demystifying analysis of the real process of innovation in building was not the only achievement of Adam's paper. He moved on from the example of the house to justify the idea of a full-blown classical architecture of glass fibre, stainless steel, mylar and kevlar and solar glass. This, he said, would be no different from the continued use of china tableware after the introduction of cheaper, unbreakable plastic plates, cups and saucers, the continued use of silver cutlery, and the persistent survival of the too narrow standard railway gauge in the face of repeated attempts to introduce more efficient broad-gauge systems. These, he said, were what archaeologists called 'skeuomorphs' – old forms carried on into new cultures. Classical Revival, even postmodern architecture was like that – based upon a vast, international aesthetic system that everybody from the Emperor Hadrian to the Disney Corporation could understand. Using classical 'skeuomorphs' in the design of buildings not only does not prevent technical innovation – as the example of the house shows – it encourages it by disarming the technophobes who would otherwise fight it every inch of the way.

Not being a religious fundamentalist like Quinlan Terry, Robert Adam does not think high-tech composites are the work of the devil. Nor does he join the movement's principal theorist, Leon Krier, in decrying the huge scale of modern office buildings, calling for them to be cut down to historic size. Indeed he has already declared himself ready to design a 50-storey classical building – 'I am sure the Romans would not have hesitated to do it if they had had the materials'[19] – and he is so far from being a traditionalist where materials are concerned that, provided they do the job, the only thing he cares about is what they look like.

What this all means in evolutionary terms is that two important questions about the end of the First Machine Age can now be answered by analogy. The failure of Modern architecture can be seen as something like the failure of Benz's car – a perfectly logical, indeed inspired response to the product environment that gave it birth – but one incapable of adapting without the sacrifice of a vital survival function. The submergence of modern technology into a postmodern or Classical Revival skin in the Second Machine Age can, in turn, be seen as the inevitable outcome of an attempt to retain the new wisdom of architecture in the age of science alongside the old survival function of design privilege. Unlike the car designer, the architect of the Second Machine Age carries 4,000 years of history on his back, years that have embedded in the conventional wisdom of his species a physiological 'shape' that compels him to cling to the territory of individual creativity. Like a dinosaur in a changing world he will defend it beyond logic, beyond reason, beyond species survival itself.

## NOTES

1 See chapter 1. The quotation is from Friedman's address to the Folkestone Conference of Experimental Architecture of 1966.
2 Giovanni Klaus Koenig, 'How car design has changed', *FIAT 1899–1989: An Italian Industrial Revolution* (Fabbri Editori, 1988).
3 Peter Blake, *The Master Builders* (Gollancz, 1960).
4 Sir Edwin Lutyens, *Country Life*, 20 June 1931.
5 J. N. Comper, *The Atmosphere of a Church* (Sheldon Press, 1947).
6 J. M. Richards, *Architectural Criticism in the Nineteen-Thirties* (Architectural Press, 1960).
7 W. E. Eder and W. Gosling, *Mechanical System Design* (Pergamon, 1965).
8 G. Gorer, *The Life and Times of the Marquis de Sade* (Peter Owen, 1953).
9 C. Norberg-Schultz, *Intentions in Architecture* (MIT, 1965).
10 Marcus Whiffen, *American Architecture since 1780* (MIT, 1969).
11 A number of Revere Copper Company pamphlets were discovered by the author in a second-hand bookshop in Troy, New York in 1976.

12  Banham, *Theory and Design in the First Machine Age*, p. 11. In addition to citing the Italian Futurist Marinetti, Banham also quotes John Davidson, a Scots chemist and poet who died in 1909. Davidson once wrote: 'Class, mass and mob for fifty years and more/ Had to travel in the jangling roar/ Of railways, the nomadic caravan/ That stifled individual mind in man,/ Till automobilism arose at last!'.

13  The 1937 Lancia Aprilia was the last collaboration of Vincenzo Lancia and Falchetto. Lancia died in the year that the vehicle went into production, although its unitary body was patented in 1934.

14  CLASP (the Consortium of Local Authorities Special Programme) remains the most successful industrialized building system ever used in Britain. It began in 1957 in the Nottinghamshire County Architect's Department under Donald Gibson as a project to develop and diversify the group public-sector-financed lightweight standardized manufactured component school-building system developed after World War Two in the Hertfordshire schools programme. CLASP won a special grand prize at the 1960 Milan Triennale and was developed into many variants including SCOLA, CMB, Method and SEAC. Unhelpfully, Reyner Banham described CLASP in 1962 as 'the product of some sort of highly creative force' (*Architectural Review*, May 1962, p. 349). In the late 1970s, bending to the anti-Modernist trend and following a series of unfortunate fires, CLASP went over to a pitched-roof, brick-clad version, derivatives of which are still in production.

15  This genetic experiment is described in Liam Hudson, *Night Life: The Interpretation of Dreams* (Weidenfeld, 1986).

16  This interpretation of Benz's understanding of the role of the motor car is taken from St John C. Nixon, *The Invention of the Automobile* (Country Life Books, 1936).

17  Ibid.

18  Robert Adam, 'Tin gods: Technology and Contemporary Architecture', (Academy Editions 1990).

19  In conversation with the author in March 1988.

# CHAPTER 3

# Architecture in the Age of Science

*On a grassy slope in front of the targets they found a distinguished gathering of Service leaders and civilians, and Jefferis put on a spectacular show for them with his anti-tank bomb – a glass container filled with nitroglycerine, which exploded with an impressive flash and a crack. The young officer chosen to demonstrate it had rehearsed an act requiring split-second timing. Standing in front of the tank, he saluted, and then, turning smartly about, he hurled the bomb at the target and then saluted again before throwing himself flat on his face. Mr Churchill was delighted.*

GERALD PAWLE, *The Secret War*

THE REMARKABLE thing about this passage, which has apparently nothing to do with architecture, is the role of the salute. The nameless young officer of the wartime demonstration interposes it like a gasket between an official ceremony and an act of destruction. In effect he uses it to make acceptable the blowing up of a tank in polite society. His salutes are extreme examples of the 'skeuomorphs' discussed in chapter 2, apparent anachronisms, like postmodern architecture, that actually play a vital role in making naked technology appear to be constrained within cultural bounds. In their way, the two salutes are exact parallels to the preserved wings of Sir Albert Richardson's Bracken House in the City of London mentioned in chapter 1. The explosion is what the Japanese property giant Ohbayashi describes as 'seven new storeys of column-free areas well suited to the demands of modern computerised offices' – the new central section designed by Michael Hopkins to be completed in 1991. When it is complete, the whole building, like the anecdote, will illuminate the culturally consoling but ultimately marginal role of architecture in the age of science.

Unlike science, which grows by the accumulation and cross-fertilization of a stochastic pattern of new discoveries, architecture comes out of actions and beliefs that have grown out of previous actions and beliefs. At any one time it represents the sum of innumerable movements of the rudder of its own history, which is to say that architectural history is continually reinterpreted to create a rationale for the architectural present. Seen in this way all the colourful volumes on style and theory that populate the shelves of architectural libraries are little more than old skins sloughed off in the repeated process of reinterpretation. They are obsolete but they are necessary, for without this assiduous work at the rudder, architecture would lose its cultural identity. From there to its dissolution as a unitary phenomenon would be but a step, and the architect would join the shipwright, the cordwainer and the platerer in the dustbin of history.

It is to avoid this ever-possible fate that architectural theory, architectural criticism and architectural polemic exist. It is their job – whenever the principles of architecture become unclear – to move the rudder of history until they can be understood again. In periods of deep uncertainty these movements can often cause the principles to describe a circle, as they are doing today, before the past once again falls into place. That is what happened 2,000 years ago when the theorists of the ancient world convinced themselves that Classical architecture was the progressive refinement of prehistoric construction. It happened 500 years ago when the theorists of the Renaissance claimed the rediscovery of the Classical past; and it happened 150 years ago when the Gothic Revivalists of the nineteenth century claimed the patrimony of the Dark Ages. More recently, in a change of course equally drastic, it happened when the Modernists of the twentieth century claimed – like mutineers – that science, technology and socialism had entirely changed the cosmos so that the whole tottering edifice of architectural history that bore down on them so onerously could be compressed into a single category called the past, and cast adrift in an open boat.

The implied analogy with the fate of the mutineers of H M S *Bounty* will not be lost on those who recollect that it was Captain Bligh (the embodiment of naval tradition) who had the last laugh. Like his analogical successor, architectural history, he survived the voyage in the open boat and lived to see nearly all the mutineers brought to justice. From the perspective of the time of writing this would seem also to have been the good fortune of the academics, stylists, trimmers and revivalists booted out by the Moderns. After a period of exile (or more or less unwilling collaboration with what they regarded as the jejune theorizing of the Modern school), they too have returned to give evidence against the surviving mutineers.

That the early Modernists were mutineers is an important point to establish before considering their fate under the wheels of the inexorable tumbril of science and technology. Certainly their mutinous stance in the years after 1918 is indisputable. Barbara Miller Lane quotes Walter Gropius writing in 1919: 'The old forms are in ruins, the benumbed world is shaken up, the old human spirit is invalidated and in a flux towards a new form.'[1] Conrads and Sperlich quote Bruno Taut in the first issue of the magazine *Dawn* in 1920: 'Space. Homeland. Style. To hell with them, odious concepts! Destroy them, break them up! Nothing shall remain! Break up your academies, spew out the old fogeys . . . Let our North wind blow through this musty, threadbare tattered world.'[2] And Anatole Kopp provides similar quotations from the Russian Constructivists.[3] All of it, in an age of embarrassing kowtowing to royal princes in matters of taste, has the bracing whiff of insurrection.

The first architectural mutineers belonged to what in literature is called the generation of 1914, the men and women whose outlook was transformed by the Great War. Of course the architects among them were not mob orators or deserters, men who stormed the Winter Palace or scuttled the Imperial German Fleet – but they were ideologically insurgent. They lived through the collapse of empires and the inflation and bankruptcy of Europe, as well as the evolution of the automobile and the aeroplane from rich men's playthings to indispensable tools of modern life. They were the first architects in history to embrace science and technology as a substitute for their accumulated cultural legacy, to accept that because Art, *ars*, means skill, and science, *scientia*, means knowledge, there could be no art in the twentieth century without twentieth-century science too. Like the great Victorian engineers, they brought scientific matters into the mainstream of professional thought and popular discourse, but unlike the engineers, they took this step with all the irresponsibility of artists, licensed to find inspiration where they chose. Unused to the painstaking accumulation of factual data, they soon found themselves in a trap. Not only did baptism by total immersion in science and technology threaten their old artistic identity, but their mutinous conduct soon ensured that any escape route back from amateur modernism to professional academicism was denied them. Before they died, the mutineers came to realize that their art was at the mercy of the machine, and not the other way around.

But in the beginning the mutineers were not without weapons of their own. The general pattern of buildings designed for the same purpose had remained static for years, even centuries – parish churches for example. But that period of stability had ended in a demand for new building types. When a dramatic change of this kind occurs it is always because the needs of the user have suddenly outstripped the capacity of the state-of-the-art building envelope. And in the half-century of the mutiny, this happened in rapid succession to a whole range of major building types including housing, schools and hospitals. Even after the mutiny had been quelled, it happened to banks and financial services buildings, a field in which radical change under the impact of a new technological environment once again burgeoned forth in such structures as Richard Rogers's Lloyd's building or Norman Foster's Hongkong and Shanghai Bank. Taken as a whole, an explosion of demand for new serviced floorspace coincided with the Modern mutiny and its aftermath. It created unorthodox opportunities for the architects of the financial services buildings in the 1980s in exactly the same way as it created possibilities for the inventors of prefabricated building systems in the 1940s. Then and now, the key to professional survival was the ability to make these opportunities and possibilities culturally acceptable. The price of failure was not that these opportunities would go away, but that they would be seized by aliens outside the culture of architecture, and thus form another professional power base in the built environment.

Throughout the history of building since the Industrial Revolution there

**51**   Tipton lock-keeper's cottage, 1830. The first recorded metal prefabricated house.

has been a *leitmotif* of artless, technological structures, far in advance of their time but disregarded by the culture of architecture because they failed, in the sense of the quotation at the head of this chapter, to salute before they went off. It is these structures whose cumulative effect has been to usher into existence a complex, multi-disciplinary space-enclosing technology based upon a network of expert subcontracting component suppliers. It is not generally recognized that it is the combined impact of all these spurned architectural innovations that has created the present demarcation between the superficial architecture of the image and the technological possibilities of the envelope that the greatest 'high-tech' masters can achieve today.

The prefabricated cast iron lock-keeper's cottage at Tipton Green, Staffordshire, is a case in point. Consisting of a series of flanged full-height wall panels bolted together it was first erected before 1830 as a toll house on the West Bromwich–Birmingham highway; then it was unbolted in 1870 and moved to Tipton, where it remained in use until it was unbolted again and demolished in 1926. This 'unobtrusive and almost unrecorded building', as its chronicler wrote in 1946, was not simply the first prefabricated metal house in the history of the world, but the prototype for generations of cladding systems that are now universally the preserve of specialist manufacturers rather than architects.[4]

Scarcely better known, and just as thoughtlessly disposed of was J. C. Loudon's wrought-iron framed glasshouse at Bretton Hall, Yorkshire, erected in 1827 with a dome spanning more than 16 metres. This structure depended

**52**   Richard Turner's wrought-iron Palm House at Kew, 1844–8. Built in defiance of an impractical monstrosity conceived by his architect.

**53**   The Crystal Palace, 1851. Sir Joseph Paxton's pre-emptive masterpiece of component design and project management.

for its rigidity on the interaction of glass and iron, thus for the first time substituting the precision assembly of manufactured components for sheer mass to achieve structural strength. Loudon was a gardener, and little of his work has survived. A better-known glasshouse, the Palm House at Kew by Richard Turner with Decimus Burton, built in 1844, fared better, but only at the price of a battle for supremacy between its real creator, the ironfounder Richard Turner, and the architect Burton. Turner only succeeded in getting his light wrought-iron design built by tendering for a cast iron structure four times as heavy that had been designed by Burton – a structure he abandoned before construction began. In its original constructed form the Palm House boasted thermic welding and post-tensioning, both used for the first time and subsequently 'rediscovered'. In the fullness of time the construction of conservatories, like the design of the curtain walling systems developed from them, was also to move from the ambit of the architect to the catalogue of the specialist supplier.

The logical successor to the Palm House was Sir Joseph Paxton's Crystal Palace of 1851, an epic of prefabrication, standardization, precision and construction management unprecedented in its time and hardly matched since.[5] This building, although it no longer exists, cannot by any stretch of the imagination be described as unknown, but it has in common with Tipton and the earlier glasshouses the fact that it made no contact with the mainstream of architectural development at the time of its construction. Indeed one might see, in its rapid removal from Hyde Park to Sydenham at the end of the 1851 Great Exhibition, something of the jealousy and displeasure that always greets a display of technological mastery that has not been properly introduced.

The Crystal Palace is now widely acknowledged to have been less innovative in terms of long spans, iron construction and the use of glass, than in its rationalization of components and its project management – both of which permitted the design and construction of nearly one million square feet of floorspace on three floors in only nine months. Subsequently both these skills, component design and project management, have also largely slipped out of the grip of architecture into the specialized operations of the construction industry.

Much more modest than the Palm House, and insignificant in size beside its revolutionary successor, was the complete embodiment of the modern steel frame that is to be found in the four-storey Sheerness Boat Store of 1858, designed by the Admiralty engineer Godfrey Greene. With neither diagonal bracing nor sheer walls, this wrought and cast iron frame building depended entirely for its stability on the stiffness of the bolted joints between its columns and beams. Even today its galvanized corrugated iron and glass cladding gives it the appearance of an industrial or military building of at least two generations later. It resembles in fact the prototype of precisely the kind of design-and-build light industrial or science park structure that today is routinely erected

**54** Sheerness Boat Store 1858–60. Clad in glass and corrugated iron, it was the precursor of all modern light industrial sheds.

alongside motorways without the intervention of any architect at all – except perhaps in connection with landscaping.

Even more humble than the Sheerness Boat Store was the pioneer reinforced concrete work of W. B. Wilkinson, a Newcastle plasterer. In 1854 Wilkinson patented a form of reinforced concrete floor construction using Portland Cement, permanent shuttering and draped steel wire hawsers as reinforcement. His patent antedated Coignet's and Monier's first English patents for iron-reinforced concrete construction, and he carried out a considerable amount of building work in Northern England, but his work lay dormant, even though it was executed 30 years before the same system was imported from France in the 1890s to form the basis of all subsequent reinforced concrete frame buildings. A cottage built by Wilkinson in Newcastle in 1865 was demolished in 1955 and occasioned some belated architectural interest in his work,[6] but the design and detailing of concrete structures is no longer regarded as part of the work of an architect.

The Garden City movement has rightly never been seen as a powerhouse of technological innovation, but it too boasts at least one pioneering obscurity. At Letchworth a precast concrete cottage was built as a competition entry in 1904.

**55**  A Wilkinson reinforced concrete house built in Newcastle in 1865. It antedated French patents by 30 years.

**56**  Letchworth precast concrete house by J. Brodie, 1904. Despite its conventional appearance, it anticipated the system-building boom by 50 years.

**57** The Nissen hut was patented by a Canadian engineering officer in 1916. This American house version was mass-produced for export by the Great Lakes Steel Corporation after World War Two.

**58** The final development of the Nissen hut is enclosure by on-site profiling. This 1987 tennis club in Devon by BDG International spans 30 metres with unsupported continuous arched steel panels.

Although this building still exists – being in a Conservation Area – little is known about its origins.[7] Designed by J. Brodie, City Engineer of Liverpool, its method of construction was to be virtually ignored for half a century. Like Wilkinson's pioneering work with reinforced concrete, the Letchworth pre-casting experiment served only as the prelude to the adoption of this method of construction as a specialist technique, one that was later to assume great importance in the era of system building and tower block construction. At that stage, although it had long since been removed from the control of architects, the unsuccessful use of precast concrete components was repeatedly blamed on them.

A quite different but spectacularly advanced structure that was destined to be built in enormous numbers and exert a powerful influence on subsequent lightweight steel construction was the Nissen hut. Designed in 1916 by Lieutenant Colonel P. N. Nissen (1871–1930), a Canadian Engineer officer, the 'Nissen Bow Hut' was a triumph of minimum material for maximum enclosed volume, and the first ever mass-produced complete building. During the Great War more than 20,000 were used to provide shelter for half a million men. The construction of the Nissen hut was based on the use of pre-curved corrugated steel sheets for its combined walls and roof, all the sheets being interchangeable and fixed to 'T'-section steel hoop rafters and straight purlins with hook bolts. The wooden floor rested on longitudinal sleeper joists and the two end walls were supplied complete – one with a door and two small windows, and the other with a large central window. The whole hut, which measured 8·2 metres by 4·9 metres, weighed a ton and could be carried on an army lorry. No component was too heavy to be lifted by two men and the only assembly tool required was a spanner: four men could erect accommodation for twenty-four in four hours.[8] Twenty years later the Nissen principle was developed to provide long-span 'Blister' hangars for aircraft, and even now its influence has not ceased. Today on-site profiling enables continuous-arched corrugated steel buildings spanning up to 30 metres to be made using the same 'bow' technique but – as in the cases of reinforced concrete and precast concrete design – the technique has vacated the architectural arena in favour of specialized production firms.

World War Two produced a similar level of development in lightweight accommodation structures to the Great War. In addition to developments of the Nissen prototype, military huts were built using prestressed concrete, cement and woodchip panels, and even lightweight concrete shells using fabric reinforcement instead of steel. After the war this flood of innovation was redirected towards resolving the massive housing shortage of the period. In this connection three of the most interesting structures were designed to be assembled on redundant aircraft production lines in order to make use of war-enlarged supplies of light alloy, steel and skilled labour.

Immediately after the liberation of France in 1944, the French engineer Jean Prouvé was commissioned to design and manufacture 800 emergency dwelling

**59** As functional as a 2CV, this pioneer prefabricated house by the French engineer Jean Prouvé is one of 25 built at Meudon, near Paris, in 1949.

units for the homeless in the war-damaged *départements* of Vosges and Lorraine. Constructed using a folded steel structure and plywood panel system developed before the fall of France in 1940, these demountable houses were succeeded in 1949 by a second commission for 25 prototype permanent dwellings. This second design employed a light, folded steel central column pin-jointed to a pair of steel lattice ridge beams terminating in folded steel gable ends. Roof and wall cladding consisted of insulated aluminium/glass fibre sandwich panels which were bolted into position. Anticipated further orders for this dwelling type to take advantage of redundant aircraft production capacity were not forthcoming, and the 25 erected remain as the nucleus of the Paris suburb of Meudon.[9] Today pressed metal construction, too, has become a specialized design-and-build industry, with few architects or structural engineers competent to enter it.

The British AIROH house (Aircraft Industry Research Organization on Housing) was designed during the war by an industry task force, and its prototype was assembled by the Bristol Aeroplane Company, which also produced a light alloy school.[10] The prototype AIROH house not only used aluminium sheet and sections riveted together – the material and method of the

**60** ARCON asbestos-clad prefabricated houses on an estate at Great Yarmouth; 46,000 were completed between 1945 and 1948.

then aircraft industry – but its final assembly was completed using 'root joints' like those used to join the wings of aircraft to their fuselages. Even its electric wiring was installed in a loom, as in a car body, with the circuits completed by plug and socket attachments. In 1945 the 600-square foot AIROH house, delivered on four lorries in four fully equipped and decorated sections, weighed 10 tons, all told, and was intended to be produced at the rate of one every twelve minutes. Like wartime aircraft, its SSA (Secondary Strong Alloy) construction made it 100 per cent recyclable. In the event 54,000 units were completed before the Emergency Factory-Made housing programme was terminated, making it the most successful purpose-made metal factory dwelling ever. Unfortunately the concept of a lightweight metal sectional dwelling industry died with the AIROH and its less radical equivalents, the ARCON and the PORTAL. Architectural interest in prefabrication shifted to heavy concrete systems and multi-storey construction.

Even more impressive in performance terms than the AIROH, though far less successful as a product, was the American WICHITA house designed by

**61**   The first Terrapin bungalow of 1948. Designed to retract into a single box shape for towing, this aluminium-skinned 'expando' started Terrapin on the route to figure 98.

Richard Buckminster Fuller. Intended for production at the rate of 1,000 every week from January 1947 on Beech Aircraft Corporation production lines, this revolutionary structure provided 800 square feet of serviced floorspace for a weight of only four tons.[11] All the components of the house fitted into a reusable stainless steel shipping cylinder. Construction was based on a circular, double curvature sheet aluminium roof suspended from a 23-ft mast of stainless steel tubes, with the walls suspended from the roof and braced back to the mast through the floor. The roof was in effect a self-supporting monocoque structure without trusses or bracing of any kind. Requiring only a single pad foundation, the house was topped by a rotating ventilator and boasted two bathrooms at a time when more than one third of all American houses had no piped sanitation at all. Its intended sale price was to have been $6,500 (£1,300) – a figure approximately equal to the cost of the much smaller AIROH house in Britain. Unfortunately only two prototypes were built. The ambitious and widely publicized production plans were abandoned in 1946, when the Beech Aircraft Corporation withdrew financial support. The geodesic dome, the

**62(a)** LEFT The assembly line at the Beech Aircraft Corporation, Wichita, Kansas in March 1945.
**62(b)** ABOVE Where Richard Buckminster Fuller proposed to build 200 of these prefabricated WICHITA houses every day.

direct descendant of the WICHITA house in Buckminster Fuller's *oeuvre*, proved far more successful in attracting investment and clients, with no less than 12,000 in use by 1970. But with the exception of a small number of handcrafted versions its development did not involve the architectural profession.

In the 40 years since World War Two there have been other structures of equal importance that have been accorded equal disdain. In 1960, Mickleover Transport, a London plastics company, produced prefabricated glass fibre capsule signal boxes for British Railways. Two years later they marketed a panellized glass fibre two-storey office building.[12] Coupled with some development of glass fibre-reinforced cladding panels for steel and concrete frame buildings during the following decade, this line of development eventually fell foul of the 1974 oil embargo and the resultant massive increase in the price of all petroleum-derived plastics. Prototype glass fibre housing units intended for use in the New Town of Milton Keynes were abandoned at that time.[13] Today the most advanced design work using these materials is no longer directed towards the construction industry at all, but is concentrated in the leisure, automotive, aerospace and boat-building sectors of the economy.

Another area of fruitful innovation and experiment that was rejected by the architectural profession grew up alongside the counter-culture movement of

**63** A 'Drop City' dome in New Mexico, 1965. Counter-culture experiments with passive solar heating anticipated energy crisis architecture by several years.

the 1960s in the United States. Primitively hand-crafted though they were, the dwelling and meeting houses of 'the movement' were often remarkable achievements in Fullerian geometry[14] and the efficient use of materials. Countless structures based on geodesic domes, on the passive use of solar energy, on the use of industrial and consumer wastes for building, and for fully recyclable structures designed to conserve the energy embodied in manufactured products and components[15] came into existence during the 1960s and the 1970s – most of them to disappear in the orgy of house-price speculation that was to put a stop to innovation in housing design at the end of the decade.

On the theoretical front, as the failure of the Archigram Group proves, problems of credibility dogged all attempts during this period to separate technological ingenuity from the ritual obeisances required by the architectural establishment. Between 1961 and 1967 this loose alliance of five principal partners produced a dazzling array of projects based on the transfer of ideas from the world of technology and science.[16] Their projects for impermanent, decentralized, technological living environments drew freely on the materials and methods published in connection with the contemporaneous Apollo programme. Ultimately none of them came to fruition except in the context of the market for architectural drawings, where most of the original designs were subsequently sold. Comparable in their predictive authority with the 1914 drawings of Sant Elia and Chiattone – drawings which, like the famous

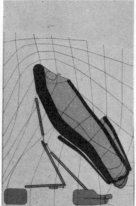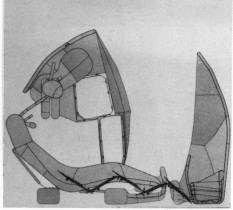

**64**   The 'Cushicle' (air-cushion tricycle) by Michael Webb. A 1966 Archigram project for a mobile dwelling.

manifesto of the former, might be said to be the first decisive events of the great mutiny itself – these projects failed to attract the kind of industrial market support that once underpinned the link between visionary concrete construction and large-component system building. With the development of the speculative investment market in housing after the energy crisis of 1974, Archigram's original *raison d'être* disappeared and the group abandoned its search for real clients to concentrate exclusively on the art market.

The lesson of Archigram's failure to attract investment is that no conceptual architecture of technology can succeed without the support of an industrial base – any more than any isolated technological experiment by industry that may have architectural implications can expect to break into the hermetically sealed world of architectural culture without strong academic and critical support.

In the 1960s the nascent aerospace industry itself survived on public funding and lacked anything that might be described as surplus production capacity to support 'lifestyle' experiments in architecture. What Archigram tried to do was to swing the cultural boom over against the wind of construction investment. In doing so it not only found itself opposed by the full force of the heavyweight permanent construction industry, but robbed even of the support of the architectural establishment and its attendant art-historical architectural value system.

The contrast between the idea of Archigram's lightweight, transitional architecture and the heavyweight, high-tech, late Modern architecture of, say, Norman Foster or Richard Rogers is instructive. Conceived ten years later than the best-known Archigram projects, Richard Rogers's Lloyd's Building was designed as a permanent, flexibly serviced enclosure that promised a 50-year capability to withstand developments in information technology. A truer diagnosis of the problem that brought forth the Lloyd's building would have led to the conclusion that only short-life, temporary or mobile expedients could cope with the mushrooming space needs of the financial services industry whose information technology requirements were growing exponentially – but such advice would have produced no £150 million masterpiece. Instead it might have generated a demand for something more like a fleet of Archigram-style developments of the military command vehicle – nowadays just beginning to emerge from the design studios of the automobile industry in the form of the electronically communicating private car.[17]

Logical as it might have been, such a drastic departure was not possible when Lloyd's was conceived. Not only had Archigram already ceased to exist when the very commission that its vision of the future had directed it towards swam into the realm of the possible, but the force of the world's leading

**65** 'Sleek Building' by Peter Cook, 1978. A later Archigram styling exercise predictive of the 'Gothic solution'.

insurance conglomerate, coupled with the market strength of the cement and concrete industry, was pointing in another direction. The phantom Archigram alternative would never even have been considered. Archigram thinking might have offered temporary, flexible enclosure to a pattern adumbrated 20 years before and still been ahead of the game; but by then it had already failed in every market-place except the art gallery. Richard Rogers offered what was described as 'flexible servicing' for a heavy concrete frame structure squarely in a tradition of architectural permanence – and succeeded.

This degree of dislocation between problem definition and the permissible range of architectural solutions is not uncommon, but it is seldom so dramatically played out at such great expense. The construction of the Crystal Palace would never have been attempted along the lines of the Lloyd's building. Its eight years' gestation alone would have ensured that it would have been dismissed out of hand.

With one or two exceptions during the brief hiatus of the Modern mutiny, all architects and architectural historians have been dedicated to the conservation of a culture of architecture that is founded upon the principle of permanent buildings with inflexible envelopes.[18] Because of this there is a firm line in the response of the architectural establishment to technical innovation from the date of the earliest 'fireproof' iron-reinforced mill floors of the early nineteenth century, to the most recent experiments in articulation and miniaturization.

**66**  IT-equipped car visualized by Philip Castle, 1988. Perhaps closer to Webb's 'Cushicle' of a quarter of a century before than any of the later Archigram 'gallery' projects.

W-M-69

One hundred and fifty years ago John Ruskin argued that an architecture of glass and iron was 'eternally impossible': more than a century later Quinlan Terry argued that Modern architecture was 'the work of the devil'. In this context it is hardly surprising that the Tipton cast iron house of 1830 operated unremarked for a century; that the great glasshouses in their turn were either built by gardeners, ironmasters, or in defiance of the instructions of their architects; that the Crystal Palace was described by Augustus Pugin, the arch-Victorian romantic as a 'glass horror', a 'crystal humbug' and a 'glass monster as friendly and intimate as Salisbury Plain';[19] that the Sheerness Boat Store languished unrecognized; and that the unique features of Wilkinson's rein-forced concrete buildings were noted only when a sharp-eyed scholar saw one of them being demolished.

In 1917 the *Architects' and Builders' Journal* noted of the Nissen hut: 'This is a reversion to type, to the type of the beaver's hut or the Eskimo's igloo.' Of the huge airship hangars, miracles of engineering, built by the Germans to house their Zeppelins the RIBA Journal of 1920 said: 'It might be imagined that the engineer who originated this type sought inspiration from his umbrella.'[20] Twenty-five years later the *Architects' Journal* described the AIROH as 'this tin-can house'[21] and noted that it had 'little in its appearance to recall the taut lines of the Spitfire'. When Richard Buckminster Fuller offered the original drawings of his revolutionary Dymaxion house to the American Institute of Architects they were sent back.

Prefabricated housing, 'the industry that capitalism forgot' as *Fortune* described it in 1947, was dismissed by the older generation of architects everywhere – not because they could not see the reasons for it, but because they sensed the underlying weakness of its political, financial and technical position. Starved of 'culturalizing' architectural support and forced into destructive compromises with permanence, prefabricated housing lurched into the hands of the concrete industry and a bankruptcy that was not solely monetary. 'When that lot falls down I shall die laughing,' said Raymond Erith, an unregenerate Classicist,[22] at the height of the 1960s system-building boom, a time when Archigram was earnestly predicting a 'flip point', where society would 'jack in' its outworn environment, because 'We don't need traditional housing when we can sink an entire living environment to the bottom of the sea.'[23] Erith died before he laughed, but he need only have survived another decade.

Alison and Peter Smithson might naively write in the report that accompanied their 1951 Coventry Cathedral competition entry: 'Modern Architecture has at its disposal means of expression which would have sent Brunelleschi wild with joy', but their view was held only by a minority of the profession. In the event, seizing upon the means of expression that would have sent Brunelleschi wild, and yet at the same time making them culturally

**67** OPPOSITE 'A mobile wall-building machine of the year 2036' as envisaged for the 1936 Alexander Korda film *The Shape of Things to Come.*

acceptable proved to be impossible. The logic of their position urged the mutineer architects to make another quantum forward leap, and then another, and another, until a breathless race to keep up with the materials and methods of science and industry became the identity of architecture itself. But that was impossible for unincorporated professionals with only the sketchiest idea of what research budgets and testing laboratories were for.

Chiefly because they chose to remain a collection of individual artists instead of becoming an industry, the architects of the generation of 1914 never did initiate an architecture of continuous technological evolution. Images of a totally mechanized environmental industry under their control were beautifully conveyed in film sequences, like the epic 1936 production *The Shape of Things to Come* by Alexander Korda, scripted by H. G. Wells, which devoted much model-making time to such never-to-be-born achievements as a 'mobile wall-building machine of the year 2036'. But the reality, prematurely born in the large-panel system-building factories of the 1960s, proved unviable without the umbilical cord of subsidy, and was in any case, as we have seen, no longer the preserve of the architectural profession.

'Industrialization of the process of construction is a question of new materials . . . Our technologists must and will succeed in inventing materials that can be industrially manufactured and processed and that will be weather-proof, soundproof and insulating. I am convinced that traditional methods of building will disappear.' So wrote Mies van der Rohe in 1924 in a little Weimar magazine called *G* (for *Gestaltung*). The same not unreasonable belief surfaced outside the profession 15 years later when Professor J. D. Bernal wrote in *The Social Function of Science*: 'It will soon be possible to break altogether with the tradition of putting stone on stone or brick on brick and move in the direction of rational fabrication.'[24]

Even as late as 1962 Herbert Ohl, a German architect expert in prefabrication, could still argue in the pages of *Architectural Design* that 'While the artistic and formal interests of the last hundred years have taken the task of the architect away from productivity, in spite of all attempts to rescue him . . . the architect must realise that the machines, processes and appropriate materials of industry are the effective means for the production of buildings.'[25]

Alas for all these dreams of a profession transmuted into a kind of board of directors for a global fabrication industry. The net result of the collapse of the mutiny was a Restoration, an age of architecture populated by frightened practitioners who, in Charles Jencks's felicitous phrase, know just how far too far they can go. Where once a break with tradition was seen as thrilling and final, now creeping tendrils of sentiment are encouraged to grow over it, concealing it from view like a crack in a wall.

The failure of architects to learn design-and-build, and to undesign and unbuild, at the pace of science and technology was a crucial matter, even if despite the apparent lack of interest of their profession, the struggle to achieve this goal still cannot really be said to be over. Today, after nearly a century of awareness of the problem it poses, and with physical planning already a victim of its failure, the obsolescence and inflexibility of the old built environment has become as great a threat as pollution, starvation or war. The locking up of resources in impenetrable complexes of buildings, arguably a survival function in pre-industrial times, is now a tragic weakness.

The crucial failure was the failure to abandon permanence and monumentality, and it occurred at the very hinge of the two Machine Ages, when the power of ideology that dominated the Modern Movement died. Today there is no political will to change society through architecture, and there are no architectural ideas to bring about the changes. If politics has become an evasive pragmatism from top to bottom, architecture too has divorced itself from what science has made possible. Instead it has become an exercise in infiltration whose sole aim is to ensure that something called 'architecture' remains within the cascade of images that ideology-free consumers now demand.

Thirty years ago the ideological claim 'We are a Welfare State' conjured up images of public housing, school and hospital buildings – and thus led from an understood political ideology, via an understood application of science and technology, to an understood type of architecture. Today the mosaic of images comes first and the political idea, where it is necessary at all, is pieced together afterwards. Architects can deal with this – indeed they have always been better at creating images than providing intelligible explanations for them – but they deal with it in the uneasy consciousness that they are working in the afterglow of the last age of the primacy of architectural ideas. Because of this folk-memory of what is now dismissed as 'utopian' thought, the world still requires some sort of rationale to accompany the design of a prominent building, but it is less and less required to be challenging, and to confess that it concerns something called 'ephemeralization' instead of someone called 'Inigo Jones' is to flirt with rejection.

To succeed in the present, in the image cascade and the ideas afterglow, architects no longer work through compliance with political directives or social ideas, but through the random achievement of a state of stardom which we might define as massive image replication. The media will seize upon a name, a style-descriptor or an image that others will obligingly synchronize with what is rapidly becoming a non-objective, almost astrological reality. There is a formula that links it indissolubly with the award of commissions – 60 column-centimetres reaching 4·6 million people equals one art gallery. A 16-page spread in Italian Vogue equals one TV series. One TV series equals 120 column-centimetres reaching 9·2 million people equals one high-tech bank, and so on. The mechanism of this stardom involves not so much teamwork – too often proclaimed as the hallmark of Modern architecture to be popular in the post-Modern world – as corporate enterprise. This means that the process of obtaining a major commission is not creative – it resembles winning an election rather than painting the Mona Lisa – but it calls for a rare mixture of stamina, influence, luck and obedience. Getting into contention for the job in

**68** Scott, Brownrigg & Turner's 'Concept 2000'. Inscrutable, but a favourite backdrop for up-market car advertising.

the first place depends on being able to marshal as many influential supporters and expert consultants as an American presidential candidate. Getting the design accepted – even in the case of a competition win – depends upon the continued congruence of its imagery with current emotions, which can oscillate as wildly as the currency market or the career vicissitudes of key individuals in the client body.

It is easy to see the power of imagery in the canonical buildings of today, easier than to find the materials science that lies buried within them. It was because Richard Rogers's design for Lloyd's looked like an oil rig in 1978 – the one year when North Sea oil really looked like an intervention of Providence to save the nation from penury and banana republic inflation – that it was accepted. Eight years later it was because the building was fortuitously completed and widely publicized in the year of the deregulation of the Stock Exchange that its coil-spring staircases and stacked lavatory pods became forever fixed in the public mind as the image of 'Big Bang'. Lloyd's will carry those two associations with it for as long as it stands. Despite its much-vaunted flexibility, it is as immutably fixed in time as the Bastille or the Winter Palace.

Less conspicuously, but in exactly the same way, Scott, Brownrigg & Turner's 1986 mirror-glass Concept 2000 office block in Farnborough – which within a year of its completion had already featured in no less than nine up-market car company advertising campaigns, including Mercedes, BMW and Audi – had become identified with the privatized, inscrutable economic success of the invisible economy. Like Lloyd's sculptural homage to black gold, Concept 2000's inscrutable reflective mirror glass struck lucky as a symbol. What better to epitomize the abstract secret wealth and ultimate mystery of the information economy than the enigmatic, reflective, out-of-town complex with its inscrutable antennae and its line of black BMWs with tinted windows?

Images are the short form of communication in the age of science, and they have supplanted literal ideas at many levels. Political ideology is one, and architectural theory is another. Today images of buildings are more important than their substance, however ingeniously their substance may have been arrived at. Thus it is that the whole idea of technology transfer, which at the level of the image cascade does not exist – because it cannot be instantaneously perceived but must be explained – languishes in obscurity while Lloyd's and 'Concept 2000' are as much a part of the image system of post-industrial Britain as the exploding tower block and the cellular telephone.

## NOTES

1 Barbara Miller Lane, *Architecture and Politics in Germany: 1919–1945* (Harvard University Press, 1968).
2 Ulrich Conrads and Hans Sperlich, *Fantastic Architecture* (Architectural Press, 1963).
3 Anatole Kopp, *Constructivist Architecture in the USSR* (Academy Editions, 1985).
4 The Tipton lock-keeper's cottage is described and illustrated in 'An Outline of Prefabrication' by D. Dex Harrison, in *Tomorrow's Houses*, edited by John Madge (Pilot Press, 1946).
5 Well illustrated and dispassionate descriptions of Loudon's, Turner's and Paxton's great glasshouses are given in *Structural Engineering: Two Centuries of British Achievement*, edited by A. R. Collins (Tarot Print Ltd, 1983).
6 Wilkinson's pioneer reinforced concrete structures are described in National Building Studies, Special Report No. 24, *A Note on the History of Reinforced Concrete in Buildings* (HMSO, 1956).
7 The Letchworth precast concrete house is illustrated in *Structural Engineering* (see note 5 above).
8 A detailed and illustrated description of the Nissen hut of 1916 is given in Keith Mallory and Arvid Ottar, *Architecture of Aggression: Military Architecture of Two World Wars* (Architectural Press, 1973).
9 The Prouvé prefabricated houses at Meudon are described in 'Prouvé's Prefabs' by Charlotte Ellis, *The Architects' Journal*, 3 April 1985, pp. 46–51.
10 The AIROH house is described by W. Greville Collins in *Tomorrow's Houses* (see note 4 above). The light alloy school project is described in Andrew Saint, *Towards a Social Architecture* (Yale University Press, 1987).
11 There have been numerous illustrated descriptions of Buckminster Fuller's WICHITA house. The most detailed is contained in Burnham Kelly, *The*

*Prefabrication of Houses* (Chapman & Hall, 1951), more recently in 'Twenty-First Century Man', *The Architects' Journal*, 15 February 1984, pp. 42–4.

12 Described and illustrated in Royston Landau, *New Directions in British Architecture* (Studio Vista, 1968).

13 The most impressive victim of the energy crisis in this respect was the glass–fibre-reinforced plastic fibrous plaster sandwich modular house design by Derek Walker and Pierre Botschi of Milton Keynes Development Corporation. This and other designs are described and illustrated in 'Experimental and Low Cost Housing at Milton Keynes', *The Architects' Journal*, 25 September 1974, pp. 729–37.

14 Among the various out-of-print volumes dealing with this phenomenon are *Steve Baer's Dome Cookbook* (vols 1–4, copyright 1968, 1969, 1970) and *Drop City* by Peter Rabbit (Olympia Press, 1971).

15 A survey of the modest prospects for this last variant of counter-culture housing is given in Martin Pawley, *Building for Tomorrow: Putting Waste to Work* (Sierra Club Books, 1982).

16 The best collection of early Archigram thoughts and designs is contained in Peter Cook's short book, *Architecture: Action and Plan* (Studio Vista, 1967). The fullest exploration of the concept of a reconfigurating, mobile, ephemeral architecture is to be found in William Zuk and Roger Clark's *Kinetic Architecture* (Van Nostrand Reinhold, 1970). A much later endorsement of the importance of these ideas and this period is to be found in Heinrich Klotz, *The History of Post-Modern Architecture* (MIT Press, 1988).

17 A full discussion of the limited range of issues relating to obsolescence that did play a part in the design of the Lloyd's building is to be found in *Architectural Review* for October 1986, *The Architects' Journal* for 22 October 1986, and *L'Architecture d'Aujourd'hui*, No. 247, October 1986.

18 The surprising extent of the unanimity surrounding this opinion was evidenced by the support Richard Rogers gave to the campaign to prevent the overcladding of the Erno Goldfinger buildings at the Elephant and Castle. See chapter 1.

19 The above quotations are taken from J. Mordaunt Crook, *The Dilemma of Style* (John Murray, 1988).

20 Cited in Mallory and Ottar, *Architecture of Aggression* (see note 8 above).

21 Richard Sheppard in *The Architects' Journal* , 18 January 1945.

22 Quinlan Terry recalled this observation in conversation with the author in 1985.

23 Astragal, *The Architects' Journal*, 3 November 1967.

24 Both quotations are from Saint, *Towards a Social Architecture*.

25 Herbert Ohl, director of the short-lived Hochschule fur Gestaltung at Ulm, quoted in *Architectural Design*, April 1962, p. 162.

# CHAPTER 4

# Energy, the Great White Hope

*Cambridge researchers are soon to put to the test their claim that there is
enough energy in the air to heat and run a home in the damp and chill of an
English winter. Mr Alexander Pike, head of the technical research
division at the university said, 'We are not eco-freaks. We are trying to
establish a firm theoretical framework before we start building hardware.'*

> *The London Evening Standard*, 15 March 1974

ON 6 October 1973, when the Egyptian army crossed the Suez Canal and
began the train of events that was to culminate in a quintupling of the price of
Arab oil and the spectre of fuel starvation in the United States, the theory of
functional design and the reputation of Modern architecture were both in
eclipse. But if we accept for one moment Charles Jencks's citation of 15 July
1972 at 3.32 p.m. as the date when Modernism slipped into a coma, even if it
did not actually die, then 6 October 1973 at 2.05 p.m. was the date when a
massive shock was administered to its inert form that almost brought it back to
life.

The energy crisis almost saved Modern architecture. For a few years after
the Yom Kippur War it really looked as if a dramatic, design-liberating
discipline for buildings, more stringent than the rationalization demanded by
the prefabricators of 30 years before, yet with all the added potential of another
30 years of scientific and technological innovation, was back with a vengeance.
If energy was once again to be as scarce and expensive as it had been during the
Second World War and its aftermath, then the same kind of limitless ingenuity
would have to be used in regulating its consumption by building. Extrava-
gance was the original charge against, and may always be the Achilles heel of
postmodern architecture. Its unrestrained use of the entire cosmos of formal
architectural symbols; its frivolous multiplication of the surface area of the
building envelope; its prodigal use of unnecessary building materials; its
indifference to engineering economy; its extravagant use of land and its
irrational dedication to whim and history instead of restriction and allocation –
all of this is in direct opposition to the shatteringly simple argument that usable
energy resources are finite, and 'stylistic' architecture is an excessive consumer
of energy.

The energy crisis meant that overnight the Modernists were awarded a
poker hand that at first sight looked as certain to win as had functionalism
during the desperate shortages of the years of conflict. No amount of

monumental posturing or historical mumbo-jumbo could come up with an answer to the energy crisis: this was the real thing. It called for large doses of more-for-less new technology.

By 1974 the United States faced a situation it had not confronted since 1942: a nation that had grown used to being rich and omnipotent suddenly knew what it was like to be threatened; at the same time the nations of Europe, which had merely been poor, suddenly saw destitution staring them in the face. Unlike the situation in 1942, when the country had been an energy exporter on a world scale, the United States was now desperately short of the very commodity that had assured the Allies victory over the Axis powers. The truth was that United States domestic oil production had peaked a bare three years before the fourth Arab–Israeli war, at a time when nearly 40 per cent of the petroleum consumed in the United States was already being imported from overseas. In Japan and Western Europe the position was even worse. With North Sea Oil not yet on stream, Europe's dependence on Middle East sources had been steadily growing since World War Two. The Arab oil embargo could not have been better timed or more selectively employed, and the result was that the then six painstakingly assembled nations of the European Community instantly fell apart. Confronted with oil starvation, no concerted energy policy was possible and the EEC temporarily collapsed into an unedifying series of unilateral deals with Arab suppliers. When the facts about oil imports sank in, every newspaper columnist in the Western World assured his or her readers that the age of cheap energy was over and, unless they took the energy crisis seriously, the result would be 'the heat death of the universe'.

Against this apocalyptic background the battle of architectural styles might have seemed trivial, but it was not. As soon as the grim outlines of the 1974 energy crisis were clear, the United States government embarked on a number of urgent computer studies intended to produce 'snapshots' of energy movement through the national economy to form the basis for future energy rationing, should it become necessary. One of the most important of these studies was a report published in 1977 under the title *Energy Use for Building Construction*. The EBC Report, as it came to be known, was compiled by an Energy Research Group at the University of Illinois and a New York firm of architects headed by Richard Stein.[1] What it showed was that construction was a vast consumer of energy, gulping down 10 per cent of all the energy annually consumed in the United States, and that over 80 per cent of this energy was embodied energy, the energy tied up in the materials and components that architects and engineers selected or rejected when they designed buildings.

According to the EBC Report, of the 70 trillion kilowatt hours of energy consumed annually by construction in the United States in the early 1970s, 50 per cent went into new building, 40 per cent into civil engineering projects, and only 10 per cent into maintenance and repair. Depending on the type of new building, the embodied energy consumed could range from 200 kWh per square metre – in the case of science laboratories – to only 50 kWh in the case of warehousing. New single-family detached housing, at 100 million square feet the largest single category of building that accounted for 30 per cent of all new serviced floorspace, consumed no less than 70 kWh per square metre per year. All told, the construction sector was capable of burning the equivalent of 2 billion barrels of oil every year.

The EBC Report made three major policy recommendations for the reduction of energy consumption in construction. None of them involved passive or active solar design, energy conservation in existing buildings, higher standards of insulation or alternative energy sources. The first recommendation was that the Federal Government should issue guidelines that would require the substitution of components or structural assemblies using less embodied energy for components or assemblies using more. At the level of domestic construction, for example, this would have put a stop to the brick skinning of timber-frame buildings (11·9 kWh per square metre) in favour of wood shingle outer cladding, which embodies only a quarter of the energy (3·2 kWh per square metre) for the same thermal performance. On a larger scale it would have begun a new emphasis on concrete construction in the United States, with reinforced concrete frame multi-storey buildings consuming only 17·2 kWh per square metre instead of 29·3 kWh for the more popular steel-framed structures.

The second recommendation was for intensive energy conservation by the major building material producers in their own manufacturing processes, as well as rationalization of their distribution radii so as to avoid attenuated deliveries to distant building sites.

The third recommendation concerned design exclusively. It was that the Federal Government should fund intensive research into space-enclosing structures so as to produce more efficient building envelopes that would consume less building material to enclose the same internal space.

In effect what the EBC Report was calling for was a renewal of the kind of control over the use of energy resources that had been exercised involuntarily in the pre-industrial era – by the limitations of animate energy – and had not been exercised as a matter of policy since World War Two. But it was inviting more than that. It was asking for a level of ingenuity and innovation in the provision of low-energy shelter that could have bypassed all the stylistic and legal plot-size conventions that the Modern Movement had left untouched. To make sure the penny dropped, the report recommended that in all cases of competitive tendering for new buildings for the Federal Government, the embodied energy content of the different designs should be calculated and submitted for comparison, and the lowest energy consumer – provided it satisfied other aspects of the programme – should be selected. As the report pointed out, taken together these were three routes to low energy consumption: through material and component selection; through supplier economies; or through basic design. And it was in the area of basic design that the largest savings were expected to be made because, although they were to be confined to the public sector, these guidelines would rapidly have permeated the private sector too, for it was assumed that there would be no general energy subsidies available.

If these recommendations had been brought into effect, one of their most certain side-effects would have been the instantaneous transformation of architectural design from a volatile craft into a science. How else would the 'aesthetic speculators' of the drawing board[2] have come to terms with this new system of rules than by substituting a pocket calculator for their subjective judgement, and rapidly reacquainting themselves with the works of Richard Buckminster Fuller? For it was Fuller who had pointed out only three years before the Yom Kippur War that America had reached its then relatively comfortable situation almost entirely through the spin-off from vast research and development expenditures on defence over the preceding 60 years. How much more efficient could the United States economy have been, Fuller had asked,[3] if this research expenditure could be aimed directly at 'livingry' (as opposed to 'weaponry') through a comprehensive design science? What the EBC Report called for, unsuccessfully as it turned out, was 'design science' in place of styling.

In the event, the energy crisis proved to be both less acute and more ambiguous than was expected in the winter of 1973–4. While a severe exogenous shock was felt by all the Western economies, once the actual embargo period came to an end, oil supplies from the Middle East resumed at a vastly increased cost. Severe recession coupled with high inflation, a massive increase in international debt, and an ingenious process of 'recycling' the Arab oil earnings back into investment in the West, proved a more palatable alternative than the reimposition of wartime controls and a new era of 'real' design.

For a time large amounts of research money were expended on the whole question of energy consumption in building, in Japan and Europe as well as the United States and Canada, but it was rapidly discovered that any design regulation of new construction would have virtually no immediate effect. Because of the low productivity of the construction industry all over the world, long-term strategic measures, like those recommended by the EBC Report to reduce the energy cost of new buildings, were less immediately useful than programmes targeted at the operating cost of the vast mass of millions of buildings already in existence. Even at the levels of productivity achieved in the early 1970s, the construction industries of the developed world were incapable of adding more than 0·5 per cent to their total building stock in a year. In terms of practical politics the energy battle in construction had to be fought in a fixed environment, not on a production line. Governments had to deal with populations that were experiencing the energy crisis in the form of higher bills, not diminishing heat. For this reason a band-aid response to the energy crisis came to dominate the United States and the European Community.

After the first energy panic had passed, Europe strove for international agreements to secure oil supplies and conservation measures to limit their cost. At the first International Symposium on Energy Conservation in the Built Environment held in Paris in 1976, ten nations from North America and Western Europe, between them accounting for about half of the world's primary energy consumption, concluded that the operating cost of buildings accounted for 40 per cent of all the energy they used. The participants concluded that this rate of consumption could be cut by up to 30 per cent by energy conservation, the so-called 'fifth fuel', which would be far quicker and cheaper in the short run than improving the efficiency of power generation or diversifying its sources. At a second conference held in Copenhagen in 1979 emphasis on conservation measures was reinforced,[4] with the promulgation of new national insulation standards for buildings and an economic analysis of the benefits of different conservation measures ranging from industrial energy management systems (capable of achieving 1,000 per cent returns on investment over five years) to the solar preheating of water and the secondary glazing of existing houses – both of which were heavily promoted despite showing a net loss of 20 per cent. In the same year a study by the Commission of the European Communities[5] concluded that in the European Community nearly 50 per cent of annual energy consumption took the form of commercial and domestic lighting and heating; a further 30 per cent was consumed by industry and agriculture – with the construction industry responsible for a relatively lower proportion than in the United States at 7 per cent. The remaining 20 per cent, nine-tenths of it in the form of oil, was required for transportation. 'In theory,' the report concluded, '50 per cent of current primary energy consumption by buildings could be saved by better insulation, and 25 per cent by more efficient heating systems.'

As the tone of the CEC report suggested, the later European Community recommendations had none of the rigour of the early EBC proposals in the United States. For an expenditure of between £5·4 billion and £9·6 billion a year until 1990 the then smaller European Community planned to invest in energy efficiency in industry and transport, to research alternative fuels, harmonize energy costs, taxes and efficiency grants for consumers throughout Europe, to attract investment from oil-producing nations, and reduce the fuel consumption of motor vehicles.

In architecture the effect of this retrenchment on both sides of the Atlantic was to bring forward concepts of passive solar design, heavy insulation and alternative energy, at the expense of the real energy cost of construction – which the EBC Report had clearly shown to lie in the embodied energy content of its materials and components. Already the built environment had tacitly been accepted as inert and irreplaceable. Instead of designing new buildings that would take less energy to build, the task of the building professionals was redefined as that of 'up-grading' or 'retrofitting' existing buildings so that their operating costs could be held down. The total concept of energy consumption implicit in the EBC Report's vertical analysis of the cost of the construction industry was sacrificed to a partial concept based on the energy consumption of buildings already in existence. In so far as any thought was given to radical approaches to new construction, this too was confined to ensuring that new buildings too would have low operating costs – however high the embodied energy penalty involved in erecting them in the first place.

This is a most important distinction. Not only because it illuminates the manner in which the 1973–9 energy crisis was solved by accounting strategies that separated the existing built environment from the process of new building – whatever the long-term cost in improved energy efficiency – but because it shows equally clearly the ruinous price Western society has paid and must still pay for the failure of Modern architecture to turn construction into a factory producer like the motor industry. Under the impact of 1974, the motor industry and the building industry turned in opposite directions. Construction clung to its tradition of long-life, loose-fit buildings: the car industry developed a new capacity to build short-life, tight-fit cars. The energy crisis, that had all but brought about a rebirth of wartime design controls in the United States construction industry, actually did succeed in revolutionizing its motor industry. Where 'energy efficiency' in architecture and building soon came to mean the painstaking, labour- and material-intensive, case-by-case up-grading of individual buildings, in the motor industry the response followed the lines of the EBC Report, with progressive controls imposed on the energy consumption of all new cars so that 'ephemeralization' was brought about by design.

The result was evident in the production within five years of a new generation of lighter, more aerodynamic cars than had ever been built before, with far more efficient engines. By imposing regulations on the basis of fuel consumed – not heat lost, as in the case of buildings – the motor industry succeeded in bringing about a design revolution that drastically reduced vehicle weight, and thus embodied energy *and* fuel consumed.

Just as the motor car made the jump into mass production long before the prospect even approached for buildings, so did it abruptly end its decline into postwar decadence with the shock of the energy crisis. The correct design response, which was the adoption of the production line in 1913, came to its rescue again in the 1970s. Concentration on improving the efficiency of the total production process, through computer-aided design, new synthetic materials and a new 'aerodynamic' aesthetic, saved the motor car in the 1970s – a period when a sizeable political lobby in Europe as well as the United States favoured a return to public transport on a large scale. A massive Fullerian leap into 'ephemeralization' brought the automobile industry back to life and guaranteed it another era of real engineering design.

Building design failed to benefit in this way. Because prefabricated construction – 'the industry that capitalism forgot' – had been defeated years before by lack of investment and the high-geared property economics of scarcity and refurbishment, and so was never able to agglomerate into powerful production corporations, the impact of the energy crisis upon building was diffused. There was no General Motors, Fiat or Volkswagen in construction; no handful of major producers capable of influencing the design of a significant proportion of future production. Worse still, while at 1974 rates of production the motor industry could count on replacing its stock of vehicles in use every ten years, the disorganized, non-agglomerated construction industry spanned the whole gamut of product-life possibilities from ancient monuments, through much-prized 300-year-old houses, right down to tower blocks in the process of being dynamited to the ground before they had even been paid for.

Except in very specialized circumstances no average lifespan for a building could even be guessed at. The products of the construction industry were subject to a different value system altogether. Apart from cases like the replacement window industry, or the central heating industry, or the appliance manufacturers, there could be no direct design response to the crisis at all. Buildings were all so different and so unique that it was as though all the paper clips in the bowl on a desk were colour-coded for different customers and had to be examined closely before use. 'Ephemeralization' for energy performance in the Fullerian sense of the EBC Report was not even on the agenda of the construction industry; it was a matter for individual, and uncoordinated specifiers.[6]

Thus when the new heat loss performance requirements were promulgated, they were cast in such a form, in Europe and Japan as well as the United States, as to minimize their impact on new construction and maximize their effect on refurbishment and retrofit. Nowhere was the engineering requirement that embodied energy – the real measure of performance to weight that governs machine production – to be applied to architecture at all.

The consequence of this regulatory failure can be compared to a failure of the natural environment rigorously to determine the conditions of survival of a species. Because it was not sustained, the first electric shock of the energy crisis failed to bring the moribund body of Modern architecture back to life in the 1970s. Instead, its florid and luxuriant decomposition continued to spread in decorative images across the identikit façades that have been described on other pages. Energy alone had not been enough – or perhaps more accurately the threat of an energy crisis defused by politics and accountancy had not been enough – to transform the state of architecture. Within ten years of the publication of the EBC Report, the United States was importing more oil than it had been at the outbreak of the Yom Kippur war.

The consequences of this great failure are still with us. In the event the energy-related architecture of the post-1974 era became so romanticized that it can be compared to the worst excesses of the postmodern motor industry in the 1950s, the era of chrome tonnage and tailfins. Because the actual embodied energy consumption of construction was ignored, and the decision was made to concentrate on a passive defence against heat loss rather than an active creation of energy by other means, great opportunities were lost for making the first post-industrial connection between architecture on the micro-scale, and the macro-economics of natural energy flows in the biosphere.

Had global corporations on the model of the automobile industry existed in the field of civil engineering and building design, ideas on an appropriate scale would not have been wanting. Richard Buckminster Fuller, 79 years old in the year of the oil embargo, still retained his creative powers. Although, as we have seen, his earlier attempts to draw the world housing industry up to the same level of lightness and performance as the motor industry had failed, he had not only foreseen the consequences of massive fossil fuel consumption some years before the energy crisis struck, but he also understood why the world's economies were unable to draw back from it. In a 1972 magazine interview he said: 'The technical efficiency of our overall economy is of so low an order – five per cent – that 95 out of every 100 barrels of petroleum burnt are completely wasted.' Fuller understood the reluctance of the 'money-making' economy to invest in genuine 'ephemeralizing' energy efficiency. He went on: 'If we develop efficient use of technology we could live well within our annual "income" of wind and water power sources, but such efficient design strategies to conserve resources would reduce the "money making" spending of the global "savings account" that is basic energy economics today.'[7]

Reinforced by these insights, Fuller embarked in the 1960s on a period of unprecedented macro-architectural creativity. In partnership with the Japanese engineer Shoji Sadao, he proposed immense engineering interventions for the interface between land surface and stratosphere that represented a proper expression of the enormously enhanced technical potential of the post-World

**70** Buckminster Fuller's dome over mid-town Manhattan, 1960. Architecture on a scale appropriate to postwar capabilities.

War Two period – and promised energy gains that were as appropriate to the scale of the energy crisis as were the achievements of the great Victorian engineers to the First Machine Age. Fuller's 1960 project for a 2-mile diameter transparent geodesic dome over mid-town Manhattan, for example, created a large-scale controlled environment that was entirely feasible given the scientific and technical capacities of a nation that was about to embark on a project to send men to the Moon – besides which it offered the potential for economies of scale in surface area and energy consumption that clearly demonstrated technological 'ephemeralization' at work for the benefit of humanity.

Four other projects, all antedating the energy crisis, were designed by Buckminster Fuller at this time. The first was the 1967 'Tetrahedral City', a vast floating triangular atoll intended to house up to one million persons and be replicated across the world's oceans; Triton City, a similar built-up complex of floating concrete modules with a capacity of 100,000 inhabitants followed it shortly after. Both these projects were originally developed for Japanese clients, and at one time a version of Triton City was proposed for the centre of Tokyo Bay. The other two projects were both land-based. 'Old Man River'

**71** Tetrahedral City, 1967. A Buckminster Fuller project for a 100,000 population floating city in San Francisco Bay.

was a 1·5-mile-perimeter artificial 'moon crater' settlement with housing for 16,000 tenants around the inside of the 'crater' and a 1-mile-diameter geodesic quarter-sphere transparent umbrella raised 900 feet above it. Drawn up in 1971 as an urban renewal project for the ghetto area of East St Louis, the project enjoyed black community support and was pursued as far as the construction of a small-scale walk-in model. The last project in this category was a massive slum clearance scheme for Harlem designed to house 110,000 people in a group of widely spaced, mast-suspended, 100-storey conical towers linked by suspended motor roads at the tenth storey level and provided with spiral motor ramps above. Ground level was intended to revert to parkland.

A fifth project, dating from 1968, proceeded directly from Fuller's period of consultancy with the NASA 'Advanced Structures' research team (1963–8). Devised originally as a geodesic envelope structure to be assembled in outer space by spinning prefabricated components into a spherical shape, Fuller's 'Cloud Structures' stemmed from the polymath's intuitive grasp of the natural energy flows within the biosphere. Taking the alloy-framed geodesic NASA sphere as a structural datum, he proceeded along the same line of thought as had created the giant dirigibles in the years before the *Hindenburg* disaster of 1937. Progressively doubling the diameter of the sphere reduced the proportion of the total weight of the enclosure – plus its contained air – that was accounted for by structure: thus as a weight-lifter it grew progressively more

**72**  ABOVE Old Man River, 1971. Buckminster Fuller's slum-clearance project for East St Louis using a covered 'moon crater'.

**73**  BELOW Buckminster Fuller: spherical 'Cloud Structures' 1968, intended to circle the earth with 'many thousands of passengers'.

efficient. At a diameter of one mile, Fuller calculated that solar heat would cause such a sphere to rise like a bubble, even with 'many thousands of passengers'. By controlling heat loss at night he believed that colonies of 'cloud structures' could be made to circle the earth indefinitely.[8]

In many ways this project represents the apogee of Fuller's energy and architecture-related thinking. Five years after outlining it he wrote: 'While the building of such floating clouds is several decades hence, we may foresee that, along with the floating tetrahedral cities; air-deliverable skyscrapers; sub-marine islands; sub-dry surface dwellings; domes over cities; flyable dwelling machines and rentable, autonomous-living, black boxes, man may one day be able to converge and deploy around the earth without depleting or destroying it.'[9]

Fuller's powerful technological inspiration triggered other megastructural architectural projects all over the world. Architects like Yona Friedman in France, and groups like Archigram in England and the Metabolists in Japan, although acknowledging more readily the influence of the Mercury and Apollo space programmes, in effect worked on variants of Fuller's images of how a more efficient man-made world might be.

But the nearest to physical architecture that this ideal came during the years of the energy crisis, and also in its way the nearest to Buckminster Fuller's own 'organic' concept of architecture and engineering, was far from what had already been achieved by military and civil engineers. The scale of Fuller's proposed interventions was vast, so vast that few can grasp it. Only a non-architectural structure like the Panama Canal, opened in 1914, or the enormous rainwater catchment area constructed on the Rock of Gibraltar by the Public Works Department, gives any idea of the daring of what was proposed. Certainly the work of the 'Biological Architecture' or 'Biotecture' school never matched the reality of the giant bridges and dams built in an earlier era of energy demand. Of the ambitions of the 'Biotecturists', American architect Roy Mason wrote in 1977 – in a style at once more modest but less insightful than Fuller – of the scale of intervention needed:

Neither the smallest cottage nor the largest metropolis can ever be completely isolated or cut off from nature. What we should do is build upon this fact instead of fighting against it. Instead of expending great quantities of energy and material resources to create and maintain an artificial environment, biological architects follow two approaches: first they seek to use nature as a model and design buildings that apply the structural principles found in nature, and second they try to develop ways in which nature itself can do the construction work. We shall call the first approach 'biomorphic' and the second 'biostructural'.[10]

Despite his confident use of the present tense to describe the activities of 'biological architects', Mason's outline programme was doomed to be con-fined to experiments. Where the technological superhumanism of Archigram and the Metabolists finally ended up in the art market instead of the building

**74** A real megastructure. The 38-acre Gibraltar rainwater catchment area built to help the rock withstand siege.

site, 'biotecture' led to an isolated series of small houses and backyard experiments. There were more of these in the United States than in Europe, but on neither continent did their design break through into an acceptable low-energy lifestyle, nor did science provide them with new cheap energy sources. The Cambridge experimental house described in the quotation at the head of this chapter, for example, despite a generous research grant, advanced no further than a detailed model. The German architect Rolf Doernach, whose 'biotecture' projects ranged from a 'farm' near Stuttgart made of living hazel trees bent into arch shapes, to a proposed ocean-going city designed to be housed in a crustacean-structured dome, 'grown' on a sunken spherical formwork, made no more progress.[11] Mason's own career led to the construction of a number of 'organic' sprayed concrete houses billed as 'homes of the future', but these too resolutely refused to unplug themselves from the levels of energy demand common in conventional settlements. In cases where utopian architectural settlements were already under construction, as with Paolo Soleri's 'Arcosanti' in Arizona, the belated addition of solar collectors did little to resolve this central weakness.

Another American architect who not only belonged to the 'biotecture' school in the 1970s, but persists to this day in his attempts to, as he puts it, 'integrate architecture with ecology and energy before it is too late',[12] is Glen

**75** The BBM (Biomorphic Biosphere) by Glen Small, 1975. Los Angeles in the form of a self-sufficient megastructure rising to a height of 8,000 feet.

Small. Still teaching and practising in Los Angeles, Small embarked in the early 1970s on a project of his own of truly Fullerian proportions that is not widely known. So large and amorphous in shape that its constructional and service details were never fully worked out, the 'Biomorphic Biosphere' or BBM was intended to be an organic megastructure capable of housing the entire population of Los Angeles. Stretching for 50 miles and rising to a height of nearly 8,000 feet, the BBM could accommodate 11 million persons while the land below reverted to wilderness. 'It is like a giant hollow mountain supported on a few points above the surface of the land' was Small's original description. He believed then, and still believes, that only massive bio-architectural interventions on this scale can prevent the destruction of the biosphere by pollution and resource exhaustion. His BBM was to be energy self-sufficient from solar radiation, wind-generated electricity, condensation-collected water and hydroponically-grown food. It would also recycle all its own waste. Inside, its volume would have been so immense that different climates would naturally be experienced at different levels.

First published in sketch form in 1975, Small continued the development of the BBM until 1980. He made immense efforts to interest large American corporations like IBM, Disney and General Motors in the concept, and even appealed personally to successive United States presidents and celebrities including Howard Hughes, Armand Hammer and Robert Redford, whenever they made speeches implying some sympathy with 'biotectural' thought. In 1978 Small actually wrote a screenplay along the lines of 'The Fountainhead' in which his architect-hero eventually builds a BBM. None of this produced any results, but, in 1980, following an exhibition in Los Angeles City Hall, the possibility of constructing a small prototype using stacked trailer homes in a multi-storey greenhouse space-frame arose. The city authorities of Los Angeles, concerned over the lack of low-cost housing accommodation, voted to fund the construction of a 'Green Machine', as Small christened this prototype, on a site in Santa Monica.

In the event even this project was aborted as a result of political changes in the city government. A disappointed man, who now refers to himself as a 'paper architect' instead of a 'biological architect' in recognition of his failure, Small returned to teaching and his modest one-man practice, but he did not abandon the concept of a truly energy-efficient architecture. News of the 'Green Machine' percolated to Japan and – like Fuller before him – he was invited there to make proposals, this time to the Takenaka Construction Corporation, but no commission resulted.

In 1983 Small developed another project called 'Turf Town' for 'zoning in' the natural environment into the gridiron street pattern of Los Angeles. The project was based on the creation of four 'urban park solar mountains' straddling a street crossing and pitched upward at an angle of 28 degrees to allow the sun to strike their curved upper surface throughout the year. The infrastructure of these mountains, rising to 200 feet on the Southern rim, was to consist of commercial development fronting on to street façades – 'an intentional crass commercialism indicative of free enterprise,' as the embittered Small put it – that involved a higher than normal plot ratio overall in return for the creation of a 'continuous ecological land surface' within the framework of the city building code.

**76** Turf Town by Glen Small, 1986. A natural environment 'zoned in' to the Los Angeles street pattern.

**77** Turf Town by Glen Small, 1986. Ingenious compromise based on an accurately calculated solar slope.

**78** The Round House by Keith Horne, 1986. An energy-efficient home built in a highly modified form at Milton Keynes.

'Turf Town', while much smaller than the BBM, still embodied all the new disciplines that Modern architecture coupled with a proper attention to energy and ecological questions should have brought to the fore everywhere.[13] It was one of the last, and perhaps the most ingeniously compromising of all the true design possibilities of the energy era, yet it too attracted no commercial attention.

Apart from these after-shock projects, with the eclipse of the immediate threat to world energy supplies that followed the increasing weakness of the Organization of Petroleum Exporting Countries, the impulse toward a massive redesign of human settlements along ecological lines came to an end. The

**79** The new Hong Kong Stock Exchange, 1986. Perhaps the only true offspring of the 1970s energy crisis was the 1980s 'gas-guzzling' financial services building.

vast projects of megastructuralists like Fuller were the first to fall into disfavour, but they were not alone. Massive banks of solar collectors and projects for rooftop windmills dominated architectural magazines for a time, only to give way to stylized versions of themselves that undoubtedly helped to pave the way for the first decorative excesses of postmodernism. In the real world of urban planning, economics took over and the small-minded enterprise ideology of market opportunism replaced the visions of 'biological architecture'. At the micro-level of housebuilding, too, the flirtation with alternative energy turned out to have no staying power. Soon 'solar houses' gave way to modest conservatories and diminutive heat stores that steadily became more restrained and conventional-looking. Double- and triple-glazed replacement windows, though repeatedly condemned by architects as not cost-effective in temperate climates, and cavity wall insulation, equally frequently warned against as a source of damp penetration, both mushroomed as service industries. At the design level, orientation for solar gain became an important matter – just as orientation for the most efficient operation of assembly cranes had been in the heyday of postwar system building – and just as quickly it gave place to the non-energy-related issue of packing the maximum number of dwellings on to often inconveniently shaped sites.

But the most remarkable and paradoxical sequel to the energy crisis did not occur in the residential sector, despite the profusion of designs for 'solar houses' and 'energy homes' that had marked its coming. Nor did it concern industrial buildings, where, because process energy consumption far exceeded the use of energy for heating or cooling, the largest energy savings were achieved – albeit from a very high baseline – by computerized energy management systems. The real transformation occurred in the commercial sector where the rise of information technology led to the creation of an entirely novel building type that was faced with the problem of heat disposal as a result of the enormous heat output of its computer-related office machinery, even in cold climates. Ironically this heat disposal problem came to be solved by even heavier energy consumption for cooling purposes.

This building type came to be called the financial services building, or superbank, and its origins go back to the synergetic conjunction of Modern steel frame construction, satellite communications links between financial centres, and the recycling into the economies of the West of the fabulous oil wealth generated by the 1974 and 1979 OPEC oil price increases. Between them these three developments created the modern financial services industry out of the old framework of national banking, and gave birth to the global securities market. This market in turn created the superbank, ablaze with light and with the massed VDUs of its vast computerized dealing rooms generating 500 watts of heat per square foot or more. To cope with its information technology and its heat output a colossal allocation of cabling and cooling duct space in raised floors, false ceilings and vertical risers is required.

Ironically this aircraft carrier–sized monster has become the one real and perverse architectural creation of the energy crisis.


## NOTES

1 B. M. Hannon, R. G. Stein, B. Z. Segal, P. F. Deibert, M. Buckley, D. Nathan, *Energy Use for Building Construction* (Energy Research Group, Center for Advanced Computation, University of Illinois at Urbana Champaign; Richard G. Stein and Associates, New York, NY, ERDA Contract no. EY-76-S-02-2791, October 1977).

   Interestingly enough another of the 'snapshot' reports, this time from the Environmental Protection Agency (*Feasibility of Using Solid Wastes for Building Materials*) Report EPA 600/8-77-006), concluded that up to half the 3 billion tons of solid waste produced by mining, agriculture, industry and consumption in the United States economy could be fed into construction in the form of inert fillers, matrices and binders. Unfortunately the report was also obliged to point out that the most prolific source of this waste, the mining industry, was generally too remotely located from major areas of population to make such transfers feasible.

2  The term is taken from a well-known remark of Mies van der Rohe: 'Essentially our task is to free the practice of building from the control of aesthetic speculators and restore it to what it should exclusively be: the realm of the building technologist' (G, No. 2, 1923, quoted in Conrads and Sperlich, *Fantastic Architecture*, Architectural Press, 1963).

3  R. Buckminster Fuller, *The Buckminster Fuller Reader*, ed. James Meller (Jonathan Cape, 1970).

4  Summary abstracted from 'Energy Conservation R&D – 1', *Building Research and Practice*, July/August 1981 (B. R. E., Garston), p. 210.

5  *Investing to Save Energy*, Commission of the European Communities, Brussels, November 1981.

6  The consequences of this short-term thinking were not long in surfacing. In 1982, according to the London Borough of Camden, 20 per cent of its housing was affected by condensation. In 1983 building failures expert and former director of the Building Research Establishment, Dr William Allen, warned that the consequences of using traditional cladding materials over highly insulated interiors would soon become serious: 'I would guess that brickwork deterioration will be common in the next ten to fifteen years' (*Building*, 23 September 1983). Two years later Dr Allen warned of the condensation problems that resulted from the excessive reduction in ventilation that heavy insulation often brought about. 'Pre-war ventilation rates were about 12–15 air changes per hour, due mainly to the open fireplaces. In highly insulated modern houses rates can drop to 0·5 changes per hour' (*Building Design*, 3 May 1985). In 1989 the managing director of RIBA Insurance stated that 'as much as 90 per cent of the insurance claim problems faced by architects are associated with moisture' (*Building Design*, 6 January 1989). Further problems involving the build-up of radon gas in underventilated homes have also come to light in recent years.

7  *Architectural Design*, 'Richard Buckminster Fuller Retrospective', interview with Michael Ben-Eli, December 1972.

8  This project was originally visualized for *Playboy* magazine in 1967 by Reed Shinn.

9  *Architectural Design*, December 1972, p. 764.

10  'Biological Architecture: A Partnership of Nature and Man', by Roy Mason, *The Futurist*, vol. XI, No. 3, July 1977.

11  Ibid.

12  In conversation with the author, April 1988.

13  The BBM, the 'Green Machine' and 'Turf Town' were all developed with the aid of students at the Southern California Institute of Architecture, where Glen Small still taught in 1989.

# CHAPTER 5

# Information, the 'Gothic Solution'

*All a man needs in an office is a table and chair near a window and a few
electric wires.*

QUINLAN TERRY, 1988

IN THE last fifteen years information has spread like a virus through the body of
architecture. Unrecognized by most architects and ignored by most architectural historians and critics, it has changed its nature more radically than any
technical or stylistic innovation since the advent of the Modern Movement. To
find an equivalent period of information-driven change we have to go back
more than 800 years to the boom in Gothic building that followed the
rebuilding of the Benedictine Abbey of Saint-Denis near Paris by the Abbé
Suger in 1144.

The idea of Gothic cathedrals as the historic predecessors of the paperless
office and the electronic dealing room may at first seem surprising. This is
because it is based upon an interpretation of the function of Gothic architecture
that, to my knowledge, has no academic pedigree. Be this as it may, the parallel
casts light on the ultimate architectural impact of the information revolution of
the Second Machine Age.

There are many definitions of Gothic architecture. They range from
structural and spatial analyses to abstract invocations of an ancient and
inaccessible spiritual power. The most time-honoured definition is simply
based on the presence of a unique structural feature, the ogival or pointed arch.
In true Gothic buildings this arch formed the basis of a structural system in
which repeated vaulting frameworks of intersecting stone ribs supported thin
stone panels. The lateral and vertical loads carried by these complexes of vaults
were collected and transmitted to the ground by means of rows of buttresses
and flying buttresses. The presence of the ogival arch was the most obvious
attribute of Gothic architecture, but this daring system of transmitting load
was its essence, for it meant that the walls themselves ceased to be load-
bearing, and the window openings in them could be of unprecedented size.

This, in outline, is a description of Gothic architecture. But what is
generally ignored in favour of an elaboration of these and other facts about it is
what might be called its driving function. Clearly Gothic church and cathedral
architecture was ecclesiastical in purpose, but what did the church gain from
these structural *tours de force*, some of which were so ambitious that they

actually collapsed and had to be built again or abandoned? The answer lies not in the spectacular daring of what was in effect the ultimate development of load-bearing stone construction, but in the information-carrying potential of the key design features that its unique system of transmitting loads made possible – great height and the giant window opening.

As the Gothic period advanced, increasing height and the enlargement of the openings in the curtain walls between the buttresses marked a steady development. Neither was merely an aesthetic device. The tall, thin acoustic space of the Gothic nave produced unprecedentedly long reverberation times[1] which responded to the sound of polyphonic chanting and choral music to produce an overwhelming aural effect. In the same way the windows ceased to be simple penetrations designed to admit light, but became instead complex translucent coloured-image screens built up from mosaics of stained glass. Coupled with the still astounding acoustic performance of these buildings, what remains of the imagery of their immense windows makes it clear that they were in fact total pre-electronic information systems.

In the context of feudal society, what we would now call the information content of the religious sounds and images of the Gothic cathedral was sufficient to explain its size and proportions – in exactly the same way as the demands of the electronic information technology of the modern financial services industry explain the column spacings and slab to slab heights of its buildings. Seen in this way Gothic architecture, otherwise a phenomenon shrouded in medieval mystery, becomes an information architecture, something that is comprehensible today, its great height and spectacular windows possessing a vital information function for mass congregations.

Inevitably the strength of any such analogy with the present depends upon the hypothesis that this teaching function was important enough to make it the driving force behind the extraordinary feats of Gothic construction. What proof is there that this might be the case? There is no documentary evidence, but modern acoustic measurement confirms that the exceedingly long reverberation times of Gothic cathedrals are inseparable from their height and shape and are only suitable for the kind of music that was made in them. In the same way the content and form of Gothic windows can be cited in support. First there is the indisputable information content of the medieval stained glass that survives, or can be conjectured from remains in the great cathedrals of Europe. Second there is the physical presence in these same buildings of precisely the kind of design detail that would emerge from the subordination of structure to acoustics and the display of immense naturally-lit images.

At Canterbury, the first complete English Gothic cathedral modelled on the French originals, and in fact designed by a French master, the clerestory windows of the choir running in a great band below the high vault clearly have a didactic purpose. They consist of an immense series of 88 images forming a family tree, based on the genealogy in St Luke's Gospel, from Adam to Jesus Christ. Of this series some 45 still survive. The great west window of the

**80** ABOVE Canterbury Cathedral from the south-west. Outrigged structure for free internal space just like High-Tech.

cathedral too was devoted to a 'teaching scheme'[2] including prophets, apostles and a series of 21 images of the kings of England from Canute to Henry VI, of which eight still remain. The fact that some of this stained glass is of a later date than the structure that surrounds it, of course in no way vitiates the theory that its insertion was the original purpose of the architecture.

In support of the second contention, that the primary function of the cathedrals was as supports for sound and vision, we have only to note that Gothic structure was outrigged – to use a modern term – while the interior surfaces of the window walls were flattened and cleared of projections in order to maximize the viewing angles to the window 'screens' and minimize any acoustic baffling effect that would have shortened the reverberation time. This is clearly functional design, and it is as logically expressed in the great Gothic cathedrals as it is in the lantern-lit roof structure of any art gallery today, or in the similarly uncompromising organization of the information interior of any modern financial services building. The Gothic design imperative was the optimization of its own 'vocal' and 'solar' information system based on

**81** OPPOSITE The nave at Canterbury. All the elements of the Gothic 'solar information system' brought together.

**82** Nineteenth-century reproduction Gothic window at
Cologne Cathedral. A figurative
'narrative slide show'.

naturally amplified sound and 'coloured light' filtered into the interior through
large glass images.

At Chartres, the definitive Gothic cathedral described by Pevsner with an
interesting choice of words as 'the final solution',[3] three-quarters of the original
thirteenth-century glass has survived in 166 enormous windows devoted to
narrative biblical themes. Here scholars do not dispute that the building's
spectacular structure took the form it did in order to create huge wall openings.
The elevations of the building comprise three storeys, but uniquely the arcade

**83** Twentieth-century John Piper Baptistery window at Coventry Cathedral. On the way from narrative to digital information by way of abstract art.

and the clerestory are of equal height and the gallery level is sacrificed in order to enlarge the window openings above it. These openings fill the entire space beneath the wall ribs.

Most dramatically in France, where Gothic architecture originated and underwent its most extreme development, but to a greater or lesser extent everywhere else in Europe, Gothic cathedrals and churches were public information buildings. Their huge windows were picture screens designed to use natural light to convey visual information to large numbers of people in a way that has no better equivalent than the projection of artificial light upon an image screen in the cinemas of the twentieth century. And just as today there is no other explanation for the structure of a cinema auditorium than the functional demands of moving picture image projection for a large audience, so is there no better explanation for the structure and size of a Gothic cathedral than the functional demands of its information system.

It is perhaps appropriate at this stage to state the author's awareness that all the foregoing is a functional explanation for what is widely regarded as a spiritual, if not a mystical, phenomenon. The reader may feel that it hardly does justice to the polyvalent achievements of the Gothic masterbuilders, who repeatedly contrived to combine structure, decoration and information in an enormous single envelope with breathtaking clarity and daring. But it is as important to draw historical parallels where such are possible as it is to maintain a proper respect for the otherness of another age. The great Gothic cathedral stained glass windows, and indeed all their successors from the twelfth century to the nineteenth- and twentieth-century windows of Cologne, Truro and Coventry, are far more comprehensible as proto-photographic 'colour slides' in huge solar-lit 'projectors', with their own natural sound systems tuned by great height, than as abstract sculptures. The design of Gothic cathedrals can be understood in the same way as the design of Frank Lloyd Wright's Guggenheim museum. Conceived in 1949 in the heyday of that other information building, the cinema, Wright's famous inset spiral glazing was derived entirely from an idea of natural light falling upon canvases inclined as upon an easel.[4]

Setting aside its spiritual purpose, the physical design of the information system of the Gothic cathedral can be related to the camera obscura, the magic lantern, the cinema projector, and today's exhibition designs that employ large numbers of illuminated transparencies or video walls. If its natural acoustic performance can now be duplicated electronically without the need for enormous structural height, so has the information content of its stained glass windows been miniaturized by the advent of moving pictures and analogue instrument displays, in which the same high density of information is presented, and indeed a kind of physical resemblance can be seen.

While the information system of the Gothic window was not electronic, it directed the development of Gothic architecture in precisely the same way as the diffused electronic information needs of our own time are directing the development of our own architecture. In the Gothic era the image was viewed direct and not electrically transmitted, so there was no cabling, ducting or heat output to consider in the design of church and cathedral buildings. None the less the need for large images that could be seen by large numbers of people imposed its own spatial demands. Today the need for hundreds of individual visual information terminals leads to a different but analogous consumption of vertical and horizontal space in secular buildings. This is the best-known impact of information technology upon building design today, but its long-term consequence is underestimated. In fact it can be compared to the tip of an enormous iceberg that is threatening to tear through the flimsy hull that holds our thinking in thrall to the idea that the product of our built environment should still be architecture and not information.

Today information about identity, where and where not to go, what to buy and what to think is no longer conveyed by form and appearance, as it might

**84** Even cheap information beats expensive architectural form as a conveyor of meaning in the environment.

have been in the Gothic world. Instead a massive and separate semiological system has been overlaid upon the built environment. A visitor from Mars, asked to comment upon the architecture of the centre of Manchester for example, might well find the question bewildering. At the junction of the A56, A57 and A57M, adjacent to a bare half-dozen buildings there are, according to the Automobile Association, no less than 150 pieces of directional information, as well as advertising messages and shop or building names. To look at the buildings here instead of the signs requires a filtering out of a large part of visual scene, and in performing that act of filtration an involuntary censorship of the real world takes place.

Seen in this way, even the journey from the Gothic cathedral to financial services building is not impossible to imagine; and from the twinkling VDUs of the dealing room to the macro-signage of the motorway intersection, or from there to the micro-signage of our newspapers and magazines is but a step. In all these cases a process of selective perception is what makes the environment intelligible. If we cease to make even as simple a distinction as that between advertising and editorial material in a magazine we fall into a chaotic world of simultaneous information transmission. The effect is rather like looking at – instead of filtering out – the invasion of information that has taken place in sport under the name of sponsorship; with not merely every Grand Prix racing car plastered in commercial messages, but even the surface of the drivers' racing overalls and helmet rentable for advertising purposes.[5] To object that this process is unimportant invites the question: 'Unimportant to whom?' For just as there would be no economic flow of traffic through Manchester without the forest of signs, so would there be no Grand Prix superstar drivers if they were not allowed to market the very clothes they are strapped down in.

What we have in the modern world is a disorganized multiplicity of sign systems tracking back through time, of which perhaps the oldest and most overlaid is architecture. The incompatibility of these superimposed systems is resolved today only by the filtering effect of our own educated perception

**85**  The A320 Airbus, the first airliner with fully integrated video displays. Not that far from Piper's window at Coventry.

which, in turn, is increasingly faced with the prospect of being overwhelmed. The audible stall warning directed to an airline pilot, for example, is there because his capacity to receive visual information is already overloaded. If the pilot of a 150-ton airliner with 500 persons on board travelling at 500 miles an hour requires compressed, intensified and analytical information – a kind of digitized Gothic window in fact – so do we, the inhabitants of a rootless, fragmented, fast-moving sensory world of signs and symbols, require an integrated 'information environment' that is more efficient than a background of applied architectural styles plastered with messages.

It is the lesson of the great Gothic information system that this present state of wasteful and confusing information redundancy need only be temporary. Notwithstanding the rearguard actions of conservationists and aesthetic speculators today, the built environment will not continue indefinitely to make only grudging and specialized adjustments to the radical imperative of information. Our much-criticized environmental disorder may indeed only be a consequence of the dominance of obsolescent and redundant thinking on this subject in institutions and academies. It is only because we lack the perspective of centuries that we cannot see the 'Gothic solution' that is already emerging in our midst. If the cathedral master builders found an architecture that completely expressed the information content of their culture, *mutatis mutandis* so can we. If the Gothic analogy is correct, the next step in architecture should be a reintegration of the built environment with the overlaid information systems that have been allowed to take over its proper task.

'It is unfortunate,' wrote the architect Theo Crosby in 1987, 'that technology turned out to be such a slippery little beast, rapidly changing from a solid Victorian machine aesthetic into a bundle of wires and chips.'[6] Crosby was writing about the information revolution, something that in the last decade has brought about a massive shift from an industrial economy to an information economy. As de Marillac has observed,

While we have paid lip service to the 'Information Age' for years, we have never really understood its consequences and still do not admit its reality. The increase in the rate at which money is being earned for our national enterprises by machines manipulated by information, rather than tended by men and women, is having a far greater effect than we realise.[7]

Accurate though he was, Crosby was late with his observation. Twenty years earlier, in a remarkable insight, the American architect Edgar Kaufmann Jr. saw this same revolution not as the dissolution of a technology, but as proof of the arrival of an era of disposability – or 'ephemeralization', to use a Buckminster Fuller word. 'Technology is increasingly immaterial,' wrote Kaufmann in 1966, 'it is increasingly electronic, less mechanical, and the net result is that the imagery of technology readily eludes the designer.' But Kaufmann did not see this elusiveness as a reason to give up the hunt for the face of technology. He saw a new quarry in 'disposable buildings', conceived for a new economy that finds value

not in the object, but in how people think about it, how they get it to you, and what you can do with it . . . Within the great impersonality of the world of mass production and near-disposability [he wrote prophetically] there becomes clear for the first time the possibility of an intense personalism as a proper balance and as a proper enrichment of life. The future of design lies in *situation design* and not in product design; products merely implement the situations.[8]

Because it consists of capital-intensive, decentralized installations – not concentrated objects of public spectacle – the apparatus of the information economy has become miniaturized, privatized and concealed. For architecture this has resulted in a changed perception in which the old technology of industry has lost all cultural value. Rightly or wrongly it is no longer a source of creative inspiration. Even where, as in the case of the motorway network, it is ubiquitous and impossible to ignore, the industrial infrastructure is seen by most architects as an alien force to be fought off and delayed or diverted by local enterprise. The architectural politics generated today by the ephemeralization that Kaufmann and Crosby identify is intensely reactionary. Instead of looking forward to ephemeralization, it fights a rearguard action against machines. And even where they are invisible – as the machinery of information truly is – it conceals them within an antique shell.

The consequent final disconnection of external form from internal function is the one architectural event of historic significance that can truly have been said to have taken place in the 1980s. It marks the final shift from an industrial economy to an information economy, a dislocation that is epitomized by the international computerized micro-copying facility that is operated by monks inside the walls of the sixth-century Abbey of Saint-Wandrille in northern France[9] – and the laborious consultation of bound ledgers by as yet uncomputerized underwriters in the space age surroundings of the new Lloyd's building.

The post-industrial economy operates without an affirmative architecture of its own. Largely as a result of the technical achievements of the First Machine Age its primary energy is no longer provided mechanically but electrically – generated with the aid of invisible fuels from North Sea oil platforms over the horizon, ominous nuclear power stations located on deserted stretches of coast, or arriving by submarine cable from mainland Europe. Most of its exports are no longer manufactured goods, but formless liquid fuels, chemicals and invisible credits. Even the shrinking proportion of trade that is in manufactures consists of containers craned, trucked and shipped between anonymous depots. Most important of all, the largest single business of the post-industrial economy, the buying and selling of houses, is a financial rather than a productive process that favours scarcity. Expensive houses that appreciate in value like works of art call for embellishment rather than simplification. A

**86**  Final disconnection of external form from internal function. The old Mary Pickford film studios at Baldock, Herts., now a superstore behind the studio façade.

successful marketing strategy for them requires special design skills, not only beneath the threshold of architectural significance established by the Modern era, but irrelevant to the design of fast-depreciating industrial and commercial buildings.

Of course there have been palaces purpose-built for the green-screen jockeys of the new information economy, but these present an enigmatic exterior that masks their exciting inner world. Reactionary architectural culture finds them unsatisfactory and requires them to look either like old photographs or, more correctly, collages of old photographs using historical architectural motifs in unhistorical ways. The result of this restriction is an architecture of illusion whose deficiencies can really be understood only by those who actually work in the information economy. Unlike outside observers, they daily experience the lack of any connection between their flight deck-style work stations and the external appearance of the buildings that house them, whether they be the science park sheds in which they work, or the ornate, brick-skinned timber-frame houses they live in. The new information workers can see, popular opinion to the contrary, that their labour does not presuppose the need for anything like the lavish structural expressionism of the Hongkong and Shanghai Bank or the Lloyd's building – even though both were designed with the dedication, if not the ultimate success, of a Gothic master builder.

So far, far from giving rise to a new aesthetic, the information economy has presented the architects of today's banks and offices with a new and formidable variant of the problem that confronted the architects of yesterday's giant cinemas. The 992-line video screen, like the 35-mm moving picture frame, has no implicit architecture. Apart from the size of its auditorium, even the development of a recognizable international style for the cinema – which was achieved in the 1930s in the guise of a 'picture palace' – was a matter of historical analogy rather than functional logic. Its recognizable international form was destined to last a bare 20 years before it was rendered obsolete by the powerful decentralizing force of television and video.

Where Victorian communications technology brought forth mighty ships, huge bridges, viaducts and giant railway stations – and even Victorian information technology demanded extravagant daylighting and the capacity to handle a huge tonnage of books, paperwork and personnel – today's electronic communications operate through satellite links whose visible impact on building design need be no greater than the presence of a dish aerial on the roof and work stations on the open-plan office floors. Even the concealed 'supply side' space demands of the new technology are now generally agreed to be matters of internal arrangement rather than excuses for 'bowellist' formalism. [10]

Thus the high-tech bid to express service functions as though they were structure has imploded in the vacuum of ephemeralization. While it might be all very well to expose toilet modules, escape stairs and glittering service trunking; coaxial cables, fibre optics, lasers and infra-red signals need easy access and a controlled climate rather than a system of display. And while it is true that they cannot be too savagely kinked as they squirm their way past columns or under floors, their architectural implications are better dealt with by specialist engineers – even specialist cabling engineers – than by architects.

Where there is no overwhelming constraint on space, information already prefers to navigate a received world of buildings that have already been designed. Its technologists ask for nothing more than that the architect should be off the case before they get to work. Typically an expert cabling company representative writes in *The Architects' Journal*: 'Virtually the whole project was run by technologists and bank staff. Had it been left to the architects, this building would have been a disaster. They think information technology is a small branch of mechanical and electrical servicing.'[11] As long as this 'no-nonsense' thinking is dominant at the point of sale, we can be sure that architects will not be encouraged to enter the field of information technology at all. Apart from the need to 'leave room' for it, architects are supposed to concentrate on other things.

But what other things are there? In the age of the messenger with a letter, information meant keeping messengers, and their horses, alive as they relayed across the country: today information means codes and images that inhabit their own world within buildings, within cars, even within pockets or wristwatches. From a bare trickle of hand-written documents passed down from generation to generation – philosophers 'talking across the centuries' – information has become a roaring tide that fills the very air we breathe. Put up an aerial wherever you are and you have information; open your eyes and you have images that you cannot escape.

Most architects, even those who are successful in achieving massive image replication for themselves, are unaware of the huge scale of this image cascade, or of the irrelevance of any theoretical position they may profess to hold to their performance within it. A successful late twentieth-century architect may try to externalize a form from the formless technologies that have ephemeralized his art, for instance by seeking inspiration in those few incontrovertible structural demands that the information economy does make. The need to support microwave and satellite antennae, for example, was heavily dramatized in the original winning design by Richard Horden for the £30 million Stag Place competition of 1987 – even though much publicity about the miniaturization of dish antenna technology coincided with the publication of his scheme. In the same way the ostentatious expression of all the equipment needed to maintain the exacting indoor environment required by information processing machines provides part of the rationale for the 'inside out' appearance of the Lloyd's building.

Though often praised in professional magazines, this 'loyal functionalism' is in reality little more than a pathetic cargo-culting of the lost methodology of the Modern era. No burden of antennae, however vastly exaggerated, and no tonnage of climate control can make sufficiently challenging formal demands to determine incontrovertibly the design of a new building in the way that the mighty Gothic window did for the medieval master builder. On the contrary, these new electronic 'functional demands' can be hidden with equal ease behind mirror glass or Classical façades. The rapidly miniaturizing dish aerial can already be lost inside a Renaissance dome, the climate control equipment neatly immured in a blind-windowed antechamber.

Julian Bicknell, the architect of one of the most elaborate Classical Revival buildings in Britain, the celebrated £2 million Palladian villa built for Sebastian de Ferranti at Henbury, near Macclesfield, argues that in this respect information technology today is so far ahead of architecture that it is laughable to imagine that architects should try to encompass it at all. How much more sensible, he believes, to take a fully developed set of old ideas, like Classical architecture, and use them instead.[12] Such an approach is after all much in the spirit of 'information'. In the present state of architecture it is not only more sensible but, we are assured, more rewarding to 'plug-in' to what another Classical Revival architect, Robert Adam, has called 'the great battery of Renaissance architecture from which we can all recharge ourselves at will',

**87** Richard Horden, Stag Place competition project, 1987. But the dramatization of electronic antennae will not prevent somebody else from hiding them under a dome.

than to go on stubbornly turning the key of functionalism on the flat battery of Modern architecture.

In fact to argue that the expression of any architectural style should have precedence in design over information itself is as futile as arguing the superiority of a 'Heritage' Morris Minor over a new BMW saloon. A restored Morris Minor may be an appreciating asset, but it is no more a useful tool today than a manual typewriter. A new BMW is not only a useful tool but one that is poised (in the midst of the information revolution) to build a bridge between the home and the work station by way of its own burgeoning information technology. A comfortable 130 m.p.h. car with a computer terminal and a telephone is, after all, a serious threat to architecture. As the advertisement says, 'With a car like this who needs an office?'

In fact the role of a typewriter salesman in a paperless office is very similar to the role of even a 'high-tech' architect in a world overwhelmed by information. Because information is an ephemeralized commodity the architect cannot relate the physical appearance of his building to its physical functions except by extravagant metaphor. At the same time the confusing message of the image cascade is that he can – because an appropriate form language does exist, in the shape of the architectural equivalent to the BMW saloon, itself perhaps the 'Gothic solution' to the problem of the design of the automobile. Indeed it is true that where massive amounts of information have to be crammed into tiny spaces, as on the flight deck of an airliner, or behind the fascia of a modern car, the beginnings of an information architecture can be seen. But where information can still be crammed invisibly under the floor, or tacked in wires around the walls, the case is hopeless. Today the high-tech architect must pitch his would-be BMW building against the Morris Minor-with-a-telephone of the Classical Revivalist, and in doing so he invites defeat because he is still thinking in terms of architecture and not information.

Today a building bereft of information is dead, whatever its period. Just as a garage is a building without purpose if there is no vehicle to store in it – because the two are symbiotic – so is the modern dwelling, like the modern office building, a dinosaur without electronic information. Information, and information alone, holds the key to investment; it is the card that trumps the building bureaucracy, the *bona fides* of undisputed importance. Where discussions about style flounder and degenerate into tiny power struggles between would-be critics of architecture who are graduate geographers, and would-be architects who have been trained for nothing but architectural criticism, the cables, beams and dishes of information sweep through without impediment.

What, for example, determines the appearance of a petrol station – a building type in which information and architecture are already as nearly perfectly integrated as in a Gothic cathedral? The prototype petrol station is Mies van der Rohe's Farnsworth House of 1948, with the addition of information and energy. Energy in the form of millions of gallons of motor fuel, information conveyed in signs so detailed that they not only carry unit prices down to tenths of a penny, but can be altered instantaneously by a modem call from hundreds of miles away. Petrol stations, colour-coded in the livery of their parent oil company, are buildings made of information, clad in signs that range from their giant illuminated roadside towers to the crucial price and quantity information on the petrol pumps themselves.

Semiological robot buildings like the petrol station are one indicator of the road that unimpeded information technology would push architecture down. Another is the way that, as we have seen, it will determine the distance between

**88** The evolution of the 'Gothic solution' I. Mies van der Rohe's Farnsworth House of 1948. Note the terrace sculpture.

**89** The evolution of the 'Gothic solution' II. Esso petrol station at Heston on the M4, 1988. Note the vent pipes.

the floor slabs of a modern multi-storey office building, and the resultant system of raised floors, false ceilings and risers to provide space for cabling and ducting will determine not only the storey heights, but the overall height of the building relative to its floor area, and thus its commercial value too.

It is here, at this final non-creative level of ruthless objectivity, that the shape of a new 'Gothic solution' for the age of information finally becomes visible against the camouflage of the Heritage environment. For just as the functional demands of the stained glass information system created the outrigged structure and internal space of the Gothic cathedral, so have the demands of the world of electronic information already laid an irresistible hand upon the form of the buildings of the Second Machine Age.

Eight hundred years ago, when Gothic structure was 'dematerialized' by the need for light, the residual structural mass that held up the windows had its own information function too. The walls, towers, spires, buttresses, arches and reveals of the great cathedrals were all made to carry information in the form of sculptures and low reliefs. Because of the quantum of effort involved in carving these friezes and effigies we can be sure that they were not after-thoughts of the cathedral builders. Nor were they the result of an indiscriminate process of ornament that sought to decorate every available surface. There are bare and functional surfaces on the exteriors as well as the interiors of Gothic cathedrals; the sides of the buttresses and their included curtain walls; the slopes of their steeply pitched roofs and the upper surface of the copings designed to protect exposed edges from weathering, all these were left bare for reasons of sound construction practice. The massively decorated external surfaces of the Gothic cathedrals were those exposed to ceremonial public view.

It is this final parallel that enables us to complete the specification for a new 'Gothic solution', for it shows us how the new information buildings of the Second Machine Age can be physically bland but informationally 'decorated'. Externally their structural frame or monocoque skin will be rationally and economically designed by engineers to support a vertical sandwich of alternate service zones and occupied areas. Internally the relative volume of these zones will be flexible, and their arrangement will be governed by present and anticipated space and climate control needs. Though the height of these buildings will range from one to 100 storeys or more, this arrangement will be standardized. In general, compared to the buildings of today, the structural floor-to-floor heights of these buildings will be greater, and their climate control systems more powerful and adaptable: if necessary their cooling systems will be able to absorb very large electrically generated heating loads. Irrespective of their height, the occupied space in these buildings will be located between accessible service zones that permit rapid reconfiguration without internal disruption. In taller buildings, personnel movement will be by escalator, and goods transport will be by lifts that stop at service floors as well as people-floors. Within the occupied areas there will be flexible partitioning

systems that also provide for rapid reconfiguration, like the seating arrangements in an airliner. The envelope enclosing these sandwich buildings will be a thin, high-performance glass, ceramic or metallic skin of minimum surface area. The roof will either be flat and waterproofed with a single synthetic membrane laid over such insulation and structure as is necessary, or be part of the same curvilinear envelope as the walls.

This building is the new 'Gothic solution', and of course this description is an anticlimax because in part it is immediately recognizable. With the exception of a few details, many buildings answering this description already exist and are in daily use, while others exist in the form of projects. The smooth outer cladding of the frame version is already a common sight in most North American cities. In England most of its features can be discerned at Ludgate House, the 10-storey office block at Southwark Bridge by Fitzroy Robinson, completed in 1989. But its origin lies much further back. With the exception of the latest information technology, nearly everything is in place in the Willis Faber & Dumas insurance office building in Norwich, designed by Norman Foster in 1972. Before that, the basic arrangement without the smooth cladding that became possible with gasket glazing is present in the later commercial designs of Mies van der Rohe, notably the unbuilt 1967 project for Mansion House Square in the City of London, and the posthumously completed IBM tower in Chicago. The earliest versions of this in turn can be seen in the work of Erich Mendelsohn in Germany and the Czech functionalist architects in Prague during the 1920s. The very first coherent image of the 'Gothic solution' can be glimpsed in the two projects for glass skyscrapers that Mies van der Rohe drew as long ago as 1919. Before that its key components must be sought separately in the nineteenth-century development of the frame building, the hydraulic lift and electricity.

What we have described above is a commercial building, but all the elements of the 'Gothic solution' will eventually migrate to the farthest corners of the built environment. The first domestic raised floor will follow the 'worktop', the lighting track and the 'technology beam' from the office equipment catalogue into the living room, just as the steel frame structure leaped from the factory, to the office, to the house. The combination of elements that the 'Gothic solution' has patiently assembled over the last 70 years is already as potent a precursor as the Abbey of Saint-Denis. It is the solution to all the problems of accommodating the age of electronic information except one – the 'cultural' problem of individual creativity, the old 'survival function' of the profession.

As the single most important contributor to the evolution of a multifunctional 'Gothic solution' architecture, Mies van der Rohe understood this.

90   OPPOSITE The evolution of the 'Gothic solution' III. I. M. Pei, Hancock Tower, Boston 1970.

**91** The evolution of the 'Gothic solution' IV. Tenterden Street, C M W Architects, 1987. Take Mies and marry it to a curve.

**92** The evolution of the 'Gothic solution' V. Ludgate House, Fitzroy Robinson, 1989. Small, but almost the perfect architecture of the information age.

Earlier than any other architect he faced the fact that the new age 'Gothic solution' building was destined to lack physical art-historical features. For Mies van der Rohe to design a house, a factory and an office block in the same way was an achievement whose radicalism is clearer to us after the fall of Modern architecture than it was to his contemporaries. Even today such buildings look like popular magazines with blank covers, or Grand Prix racing cars devoid of sponsorship. Their smooth glass and metal skins convey no comforting historical message. Mies van der Rohe came to terms with this anonymity during his long career. 'I believe that architecture has little or nothing to do with the invention of interesting forms or with personal inclinations,' he said towards the end of his life. 'True architecture is always objective and is the expression of the inner structure of our time.'[13]

But Mies van der Rohe was not destined to see the final achievement of the 'Gothic solution'. In his greatest buildings there is an inevitable emptiness that cannot by any stunting of the imagination be compared to the multivalent

**93** Montgolfier hot–air balloon, 1783. An old answer, but a good one, to decoration with a low coefficient of drag.

**94** The evolution of the 'Gothic solution' VI. Future Systems: 'The Blob' 1987. Its space-efficient surface electronically informationalized, this will be the 'Gothic solution' of the twenty-first century.

visual impact of the Gothic façade. His 'objective' architecture made plain the unbridgeable gap that exists in reality – and cannot be closed by sentimentality – between the small, close-knit, interdependent society of the feudal age, and the vast, atomized, material culture of the twentieth century. But even his material culture was smaller and less attenuated than ours, for it had not yet come to electronic life. Mies van der Rohe refused to obscure nothing when nothing was what there was. In one sense this is why his greatness can still illuminate the floundering sentimentality of the present. Better by far for the conscientious objectors of the Second Machine Age that the real world of information should be concealed behind some laboriously modelled Dickensian street façade, than that they should see the bland, glass elevations of the 'Gothic solution' as they are – no more empty than a video screen, or a Gothic window.

Consider the enormous surface area of the 'Gothic solution' building alongside the equally bland and enormous envelope of a blimp. Structurally the building better resembles a rigid airship, but such vessels died out 50 years ago, and we are left today with the smaller non-rigid, a pale shadow of its great

**95**  Future Systems: premiated Paris Bibliothèque Nationale competition entry, 1989.

ancestor. Like the blimp and the rigid airship, and indeed like the hot-air balloon and all balloons going back to the original Montgolfier, like the skeleton of the Gothic cathedral or the stark structure of the petrol station, the vast, flat surface of the electronic information building is a canvas crying out to be bathed in colour and sound.

Just as the blimp became a vehicle for advertising, droning over the city at night using its streamlined surface to perform illuminated graphic tricks, so will the cathedral of information, the new 'Gothic solution', give up the unequal battle with art-historical architecture's 'vertical posture, articulation through detail and light and shade',[14] and paint its face with electronic images instead. It can do this. It can do it now. Only one thing stands in its way: the obsolete notion that, because it is architecture, it must convey a distinctive visual message through its permanent physical form. The golden age of the 'Gothic solution' will begin with the conquest of this last illusion of architectural history.

## NOTES

1 The optimum reverberation time for audible speech is of the order of 1·3 seconds. A modern concert hall might ideally have a reverberation time of two seconds. A Gothic cathedral commonly requires more than six seconds for sounds to decay. All these parameters can now be changed electronically, without the need for physical changes in building form.

2 This term is used by Canon Ingram Hill in his description of the stained glass at Canterbury (The Revd Canon D. Ingram Hill, *Canterbury Cathedral*, Bell & Hyman, 1986).

3 'France moved on, from the Early to the High Gothic, in a growth from cathedral to cathedral until the master of Chartres *found the final solution*' (Nikolaus Pevsner, *The Cathedrals of England*, Viking, 1985) (italics supplied).

4 For an account of the design ideas behind the Guggenheim, see Brendan Gill, *Many Masks: A Life of Frank Lloyd Wright* (Heinemann, London, 1988).

5 'It used to be that a Grand Prix driver's overalls were just a first-line defence against fire. Nowadays, brandishing the right badges on a triple-layer Nomex suit is the cornerstone to a million-dollar lifestyle', *Motor*, 20 July 1985. This remarkable unsigned article on Grand Prix sponsorship details the breaking down of the upper part of the racing driver's overalls into rentable spaces and the rationing of these spaces in advertisements by the use of permitted camera angles and picture cropping.

6 Theo Crosby, *Let's Build a Monument* (Pentagram, 1987).

7 M. de Marillac, 'Pioneers in a Jobless Society', *The Times*, 11 May 1987.

8 Edgar Kaufmann Jr., 'Design, sans peur and sans ressources', *Architectural Forum*, September 1966.

9 Roger Beardwood, 'Between God and Mammon', *Business*, May 1987.

10 'Bowellism' was the term originally used to describe Michael Webb's design for a furniture manufacturer's headquarters at High Wycombe. This scheme, with its exposed servicing elements, was a distant (1959) ancestor of the Lloyd's building, and a seminal influence on the Archigram Group.

11 'Cabling Guide, Part 5. Future Imperatives', Eosys Ltd, *The Architects' Journal*, 6 July 1988, p. 54. The author too has been thus advised by senior executives at Hoskyns plc, a specialist information technology installation firm. 'The intelligent building is nothing to do with the property it lives in,' he was told by one senior engineer. 'Whatever the building is like, you will always be able to shoe-horn the stuff in.'

12 In conversation with the author during 1987.

13 Quoted in Peter Carter, *Mies van der Rohe at Work* (Praeger, 1974).

14 These are the 'three principles of architecture that we must get back to', according to Roger Scruton in a talk he gave at the RIBA in April 1983 based on his book *The Aesthetics of Architecture* (Methuen, 1979).

# CHAPTER 6

# Technology Transfer in Architecture

*Man becomes the sex organ of the machine world just as the bee is of the plant world.*

MARSHALL McLUHAN, 1967

'TECHNOLOGY transfer' is a term that is nowadays used in different ways, but a useful definition that has a currency of some twenty years[1] refers to the process whereby the techniques and materials developed in one creative field, industry or culture are adapted to serve in other creative fields, industries or cultures. Understood in this sense, the process has a rich but largely unexplored history that explains connections that are too often lost in anthologies of discovery and invention.

The great virtue of technology transfer is that, by definition, it is synergetic in its use of resources. It exploits the research and development effort of the donor field in order to lighten the cost burden of the pre-production phase of the receptor field. Sometimes the transfer can be repeated, as in the development of lead alloy piping and later small-bore copper plumbing, from waterproof cable jacketing: a transfer that was repeated a generation later, when neoprene pipes and gaskets were also developed from neoprene cable jacketing.

Sometimes successful chains of such synergetic benefits rapidly build up, as for instance in the recent application of the same electronic management systems to a vast range of mechanical devices, from heating and cooling installations in factories to fuel injection systems for cars. Other examples can be cited that show a slower, more elaborate progression, meeting and parting over a period of a century or more: the relationship between the gun barrel, the pipe and the structural metal tube, for example, and their osmosed evolution into the thin-walled steel tube and the bicycle frame; then the further link between the production of tubular steel for bicycles and the revival of interest in tubular steel furniture by way of chromium and stainless steel – themselves originally developed as means of reducing corrosion and wear in gun barrels.

In addition to these more or less well-known examples of technology transfer in the history of invention, there are hundreds more in all the fields of applied science. Glass fibre, for example, was first demonstrated in 1893 as a dress fabric in combination with silk. It was not combined with resins for another 50 years. Cellulose acetate was originally used as a fire-resistant coating for fabric-covered aeroplane wings; then in the 1930s it was transferred to become the base for all photographic film. Polyethylene sheeting, like polyvinyl chloride, was originally used for wiring insulation in the 1940s; then, after the war, both were used for packaging, and then a vast array of functions, including flexible impermeable membranes for building construction and, ultimately, lifting surfaces for the first successful manpowered aircraft. Teflon was originally used in the purification of uranium for the first atomic bombs; only later did it become a 'non-stick' coating for pots and pans, and eventually a self-cleaning finish for architectural fabric roofs as big as the 5·5 million-square foot Haj terminal at Jeddah airport in Saudi Arabia, designed by Skidmore Owings and Merrill. Polyesters, combined with glass fibres, showed such strength, flexibility and lightness that they were originally used in the manufacture of military radio aerials; then, following some DIY conversions, the same aerials were sold as fishing rods; then, under the generic name of fibre glass, various resin/glass fibre combinations began to be used on a larger scale for hand-laid-up boat hulls; then hand-laid-up car bodies, baths, washbasins, toilets and showers; then larger and stronger double-formed or sandwich-construction mouldings led to vacuum-cured boats, and now a vast range of products including vacuum-cured car bodies and aircraft mouldings of great size and complexity. One of the earliest experimental applications for epoxides was in the casting of suspension bogies for army tanks: 30 years later a combined epoxy-ceramic coating was developed to fireproof flasks of spent nuclear fuel transported by rail. In 1988 the same thin coating was used to provide four hours of fire resistance to the exposed steelwork supporting the upper floors of a Sainsbury superstore in London designed by Nick Grimshaw.

This maze of seemingly random, unrelated materials applications extends further still when more complex inventions are included. Technology transfer converted a thermionic-valve 'electronic brain' built to calculate gunnery tables for the US Navy during World War Two into the first commercially marketed computer, the Univac 1 of 1950. Naval masts and warship superstructures provided the prototypes for radio and radar aerials and power transmission pylons. The flat cabling used in a vast range of computer and electronic applications today originated in a system specially developed for the confined spaces of the first space capsules. The captive bolt pistol (or cattle stunner) and the range of cartridge tools found on most building sites both originated in a weapon patented in 1915 to enable divers to attach marker buoys to enemy submarines. In the same way the development in the 1960s of a muscle accelerometer to diagnose neurological disorders was based on principles and devices originally developed to detect meteorites in outer space.[2]

Technology transfers like the above can result from the serendipitous curiosity of an inventive individual – as was the case with Robert Temple, the inventor of the submarine marker, the captive bolt pistol and the cartridge tool – or from a determined marketing effort by a commercial organization intent on developing new outlets for its own products. A striking modern example of

96   Technology transfer starts here. The British Nuclear Fuels nuclear flask train crash demonstration of 1984. Flask protected by epoxy-ceramic fireproofing.

the second category is the use of mineral wool insulation as a roofing material in its own right by the Rockwool Corporation.[3] At its research and development centre at Hedehusene, Denmark, designed by Lief Eriksen and Vagn Thorsmark, the company experimented in 1983 with a roof covering consisting of 300 mm of mineral wool insulation used as 'thatch' with no weathering layer above it. The wool, in lapped 75 mm batts, is held in place by wooden battens, and exposure tests have shown that water penetrates only 35 mm into the topmost layer.

   A similar but more developed leap of technology took place when light motor-industry-developed cold-rolled steel sections began to take the place of heavy hot-rolled steel girders for building construction. Here the take-up rate of the transferred technology clearly illustrates the synergetic advantage of the method. Benefiting from high levels of wartime production for ships and aircraft, the American Iron and Steel Institute issued its first specification for the design of light-gauge cold-formed steel structural members for buildings in 1946. By 1960 routine applications of cold-rolled sections in the USA included

**97** Sainsbury superstore, London, by Nicholas Grimshaw, 1988. Just four years to the same epoxy-ceramic nuclear fireproofing on a building.

**98** Rockwool Corporation building, Hedehusene, Denmark, 1983. The roof is 300 mm of mineral wool insulation used as 'thatch'.

**99** Freezer-truck insulating sandwich panels as two-storey cladding on a Terrapin Matrex demountable office building for Norsk-Hydro, 1983. Architect: Nick Whitehouse.

entire standardized steel buildings as well as wall, floor and roof elements, and the material was fully assimilated into the construction industry. In 1983 the Terrapin Building Company of Milton Keynes in England marketed a demountable industrial building system designed by their chief architect, Nick Whitehouse: the structural frame of the system was based on cold-rolled steel channels and, in a further technology transfer, it was dimensioned to accept foamed-core glass fibre-reinforced plastic freezer truck roof panels as cladding.[4]

Perhaps the neatest illustration of the unique identity of technology transfer as a process comes from the story of one tiny but crucial component in the elaborate NASA Viking unmanned Mars landing programme of 1976, where the problem of designing a simple lightweight soil-sampling scoop was brilliantly solved by the adaptation of a coiled steel carpenter's rule, whose dished, semi-rigid extending arm provided the model for the light, retractable scoop that was eventually used.[5]

Vital and fascinating as is its role in industry and commerce, technology transfer is recognized only as a peripheral matter in architecture. Its historic presence is often cited in passing in such isolated connections as the ancient conversion of the caps of decorated tree trunks into stone capitals; or the transfer of plant-derived decoration from wood into stone carving, but more practical examples are frequently ignored – the significance of the construction

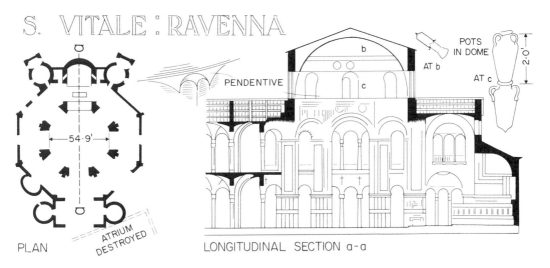

100 The dome of San Vitale, Ravenna, AD 547. Thousands of earthenware pots used for lightness.

101 'Desert Dome', New Mexico, by Michael Reynolds, 1977. San Vitale revisited using discarded beverage cans.

145

nearly 1,500 years ago of the dome of San Vitale in Ravenna out of two types of earthenware jars set in mortar, for example. The thousands of jars are completely unmodified, the larger ones even retaining their carrying handles. This structure is a miracle of technology transfer, for it predates by more than a millennium the houses and domes built in New Mexico by the American architect Michael Reynolds, using discarded beverage cans set in mortar for the same reason of cheapness and lightness. Like the architects of San Vitale, Reynolds discovered that formwork can be unnecessary if the structure of the dome is turned into a honeycomb of voids.[6]

Whether such transfers into construction originally encountered opposition or not, their pattern continued through centuries, with particular emphasis on the landlocked use of lighter, more efficient marine technology. The first cast and wrought-iron beams used in the formation of nineteenth-century jack arches, for example, were ships' deck beams applied unchanged to mill, warehouse and factory construction. Ships' deckhouses too, panellized timber cabins that could be removed to carry deck cargo, were the prototypes for the demountable military huts that came into existence in the Crimean War and the American Civil War, and were thus the precursors of many panellized systems for prefabricating houses. Nearly a century after the eclipse of the last movable deck house, the technology of manufacturing exposed aggregate precast concrete panels was pioneered by the producers of the so-called 'plastic armour' added to soft-skinned naval vessels in World War Two.[7]

Though clearly a venerable process, technology transfer in building has never been treated as a significant phenomenon in its own right. Although it can be traced through the centuries of craft-construction until, with the explosion of invention that accompanied the Industrial Revolution, it begins to accelerate to an extraordinary dominance, there is no authoritative history of its progress. All we know is that the anecdotal examples of its occurrence suggest a quickening wave-motion in time with the growth of new materials technology. The adaptation of the ribs and keel of an upturned wooden boat into a new form of pitched roof construction in the middle ages, for example, took place over hundreds of years. The first timber examples of the spiral staircase, using an adaptation of the mast structure of a ship to provide access to the upper floors of a house, date from the sixteenth century. The exhibition of a rowing boat made of concrete reinforced with a rectangular mesh of iron rods at the Paris Exposition Universelle of 1855 antedated the first reinforced concrete building by ten years, and the first large-scale reinforced concrete frame building by 40 years. Offshore oil platform frame and mast structures, developed from the 'artificial island' anti-aircraft batteries of World War Two, increased immensely in size and complexity in only 30 years – only to march back onshore again in less than a decade in the form of exoskeletal and mast-supported buildings. Even faster was the adoption of structural adhesive glazing from the motor industry in less than five years. In every case the process is identical, and each time the wave frequency of the transfer has speeded up.

It is one of the many serious consequences of the crucial cultural gap that has separated historians and theorists of architecture from the reality of building, that no early history of technology transfer exists. As we now know from developments in related fields, the next step in advanced construction technology after the glass, steel and concrete of the Modern Movement should have been light frame and monocoque enclosures using the laminated wood, aluminium alloys and plastics developed during World War Two ('Enter alloy – exit rust' as Fuller put it[8] in 1946). But, for reasons that we have discussed in chapter 2, the handful of avant-garde architects working on the use of advanced materials at that time were incapable themselves of dragging the construction industry into a pattern of continuous technological evolution. Then, as now, there was no organized conception of technology transfer to help them.

As it was, the first postwar emergency housing was expendable in all except its image – and the complete lack of thought given to disposing of it when its useful life was over. Properly speaking, it should have been made of doped fabric shrunk over cold-moulded plywood like a Mosquito, or riveted aluminium like a Lancaster bomber, or pressed metal on a light, cold-rolled steel frame like a Bedford military truck. Some of the 'Emergency Factory-Made Dwellings' – or EFMs – really were made like this, in an honest translation of the light-alloy, riveted, semi-monocoque structuring of World War Two aircraft into rapid-production dwellings suitable for the desperate housing need of the postwar years. But the EFM programme ground to a halt in 1947 after barely 150,000 units had been built. The bulk of postwar housing was far more conventional in appearance and far less creative in concept. The absence of real production imperatives to govern its design led to polar extravagances of aesthetic image-making, either in the direction of the detached cottages so earnestly recommended in the Tudor Walters Report of 1919, or in the direction of the high-rise, high-density 'streets in the air' dreamed of by Le Corbusier to utilize the air-raid shelter and fortification technologies that had so rapidly developed in the cement and concrete industry during the war.

Mindful of Maxwell Fry's qualified warning about the impossibility of developing a workable architecture if technological development continued at its military pace,[9] it is tempting to say that failure to keep up with applied science through technology transfer after World War Two was the price that architecture paid to keep the artistic integrity it had inherited from its own aesthetic past. Banham, as we have seen, was cautious in suggesting that 'What we have hitherto understood as architecture, and what we are beginning to understand of technology may be incompatible disciplines.'[10] This may be so, but the fact remains that one generation of architects – like the generation of Victorian engineers who exploited the long-span possibilities of ship-derived iron and steel – did seize the initiative offered by technology transfer, and the next let it slip away.

For the generation of Le Corbusier, Walter Gropius, Mies van der Rohe and Richard Neutra, steel, glass and reinforced concrete were revolutionary new materials that cried out to be used in buildings as different from their brick, stone and timber predecessors as a motor car was different from a horse-drawn wagon. With varying degrees of single-mindedness these great architects spent their lives developing new ways to build using materials that they had appropriated from nineteenth-century engineering and industry.

But when it transpired that steel, glass and reinforced concrete were merely the forerunners of high-strength alloys and composites grown from a science and technology leaping daily farther ahead, the ingenuity of their followers was overwhelmed. Tragically it was assumed by the politicians who elevated modern architecture to global supremacy in the 30 years after 1945 that architects held technological mastery in their hands like an Olympic torch that could be passed on from generation to generation. Seldom can faith in expertise have been more naively placed. Not only did the generation of 1914 ignore the crucial contribution of technology transfer to their own success, but the majority of them did not even think it was a matter of much importance. Taking the permanent architecture of antiquity as their model, the Modern masters anticipated that it might take a century to learn to build durably with concrete and steel. They did not expect, within their lifetimes, to be called upon to explore construction using another new generation of synthetic materials like nylon, carbon fibre, kevlar, mylar, nomex, or teflon; or to have to contend with a massive explosion of information technology within and between buildings themselves; or to deal with the electronic management of building systems and the concept of building intelligence. Even those very few, like Maxwell Fry, who understood how difficult such a task might be, did not expect it to come to pass, and had no methodology to deal with it when it did.

For a complex of reasons Modern architecture tried to ignore the demands of technological assimilation in the age of science. Like surgeons operating without anaesthetics in a modern teaching hospital, they became dangerously obsolete in their own environment. Towards the end of their lives their isolation became evident in their work, just as Fuller had predicted. Despite the spectacular output of synthetic materials and new structural technologies that marked the post-1945 period, their palette remained limited, as did that of their immediate successors. In spite of the spirited defence of their design studio methodology that is still occasionally advanced, notably by Schon, who still speaks of architects 'knowing how to act correctly in conditions of information overload',[11] it was precisely because the sons of the pioneers, the generation of Paul Rudolph and Eero Saarinen, did not know how to obtain the technology that they needed, that they concentrated on formal inventiveness rather than the new materials and technologies that were developing all round them. Technology transfer gave the first generation of Modern architects their mastery; the refusal of the second generation to seek it out again meant that they died of want of invention in the midst of a technological avalanche.

Notwithstanding Banham's suggestion that this huge defeat merely confirmed that architecture and technology are antithetical, the idea that the collapse of Modern architecture was at heart an *information* failure does throw new light on its true nature. Seen as the result of a temporary coincidence of science and building, Modern architecture assumes less mythological proportions. What Howard Roark, the composite Modern architect hero of the first half of our century created by the novelist Ayn Rand really did, was only secondarily to enjoy a final artistic triumph over critics and philistines.[12] Primarily he insisted on specifying new products, and thus enlarged the market for new materials. Indeed the financial and political support, without which Roark could never have displaced the entrenched forces of traditional construction, came precisely from the vested interest of these materials' producers. Two World Wars created massive production capacity in the cement and concrete industry – likewise steel, light metals, plywood, plastics and synthetic fibres – and Modern architects created an outlet for them in the postwar economy by rendering their use culturally acceptable. That was the irreversible effect of their work, however far removed it may be from Ayn Rand's vision of an existential struggle between truth and falsehood. With the hindsight of 40 years it is possible to re-order the data of the Modern era so as to see the careers of its great individualists as the only romantic element in an otherwise unromantic process – the technology transfer of engineering and industrial materials and methods to the design of commercial, cultural and domestic buildings.

Heroism apart, what we know about the techniques employed by the most successful of the Modern pioneers is entirely consistent with this view. We

**102** Farman Goliath, from Le Corbusier's 1923 *Vers une architecture*. Transferring the image without the technology.

know that they literally copied the design and construction of grain silos; stripped the masonry cladding from structural steelwork and suspended glass from it instead; and borrowed from the 'look' of ships and aeroplanes to create 'a new aesthetic' that was not based upon marine or aeronautical structural systems. The repeated appearance of the Farman Goliath aeroplane in *Vers une architecture* is a case in point. Le Corbusier made no effort to employ the materials and methods of contemporary aircraft construction, but he did emulate the appearance of interplane struts seen obliquely – using them as *pilotis* – and the visual relationship of horizontals and verticals – as with wings and fuselage. The ability to see complex structures in this formal, unanalytical way was uniquely architectural.

All these innovations involved cultural controversy and public debate, but their cultural significance was less than their economic consequence. They were the visible element in a resource-shift in building technology, part of the unwritten history of technology transfer whose aesthetic effects have always been better documented than its substance. While sudden and traumatic, the Modern episode was still fundamentally a political, technical and economic event followed by a cultural revolution, rather than the reverse. Viewed dispassionately, it takes its place in the long-term multifold trend towards technology transfer as the only true research and development technique that is practicable in a disagglomerated, long-life product industry like construction.

The very presence of technology transfer as a vital element in the First Machine Age – whether accepted by its theorists and designers or not – makes Reyner Banham's suggestion that architecture and technology may be 'incompatible disciplines' sound more like an excuse than an insight. For if they are, is it not strange that their encounters against the vast backdrop of history have not only accelerated, but been so one-sided in their outcome? In the end the newer technology has always won through, however disguised or delayed.

The culture of architecture is a vast and well-financed shock absorber against change, financed by the advertising expenditure of the construction industry and the huge residual values of the property market. Like the boom on a gybing yacht when the wind changes, architectural culture comes over last and it comes over hard. But by the time it does move, the sails of the driving industry have already taken up a new position.

Thus in simple terms the outrage caused by the revolutionary architecture of the generation of 1914 was not artistic but economic: it came from the business fall-out that accompanied the pent-up surge of innovation that it directed into building. After the Great Wars had caused the mainsail of industrial production to swing over on to a new tack, the boom of avant-garde architecture finally developed the power to smash the head of academic revivalism – making it possible (as an Impressionist might put it) to turn the whole engineering and manufacturing legacy of the nineteenth century into architecture in an afternoon. Camouflaged as an artistic revolution, the Modern Movement in architecture did no more than break free from the

**103** Norman Foster with a model of the Hongkong and Shanghai Bank, 1986. From raised floors to glued-on glass, the £600 million building is a *tour de force* of technology transfer.

technical suppression of nineteenth-century academic revivalism and restore building construction to its correct relationship with the new materials industries. In essence it was an episode in the continually accelerating 'genetic frequency' of technology transfers into building. Yet for architects to accept this is still almost impossible, even today, for to do so they must not only abandon the trappings of 'artistic integrity', but even the idea that the building design can any longer be 'creative' in the fine-art sense.

Such an acceptance of technology transfer as an evolutionary directive is still in the future. Architects who successfully use technology transfer against the background of a confused and deceptive art-historical culture today, inevitably do so by compromise with the fine-art tradition. Norman Foster is well known for his ingenious use of components and materials that have their origin in industries far removed from construction: solvent-welded PVC roofing derived originally from swimming pool liners; flexible neoprene gaskets using a material developed originally for cable-jacketing; adhesive-fixed structural glazing transferred from the automobile industry; superplastic aluminium panels and metallized fabric fireproofing from aerospace; tensioning devices from trailer sidescreens; raised floor systems from jetliners; photochromic glazing from jet bombers. All these and more, including techniques of presentation and colour schemes drawn from aviation magazines, are to be found in his projects and buildings. Conceptually he connects them with Buckminster Fuller's theory of 'ephemeralization', which in the early years of his office was a doctrine consciously and dramatically pursued, but in his eyes technology transfer is not a theory of architecture.

Norman Foster believes that there is a distance between this interesting but 'uncreative' process, and the fine-art tradition and the engineering armature upon which all architects lean today. As the engineer Peter Rice has observed, 'High-tech architects think that the discipline provided by the engineer is the best framework in which to conduct architecture.'[13] Or, as Michael Hopkins puts it, 'Our architecture comes out of our engineering, and our engineering comes out of our engineers.'[14]

Perhaps underlying this faith in engineering is a doubt that any other foundation for a rational architecture exists today. If the logic of structure is abandoned there is nothing but the slippery slope to Classical Revival façadism

**104**  Technology transfer at Norman Foster's 'Stockley Park Building B' of 1989. Enamelled 'frits' borrowed from car window fixing technology are exploded into a spectacular glass elevational treatment.

or postmodern irrationality. Leading high-tech architects will acknowledge the presence of technology transfer in their designs; they will proudly cite it as evidence of modernity in the descriptions of their buildings,[15] but at the same time, because it is not a 'creative' process in the old fine-art sense, they shrink from espousing it as a theory of architecture – just as their neo-classic predecessors of 70 years ago shrank from endorsing the 'formula' of function-alism or the 'tyranny' of *le plan directeur*.

Of course technology transfer is not alone in being considered 'uncreative'. There are those who believe that eschewing artistic inspiration in favour of working through all the alternatives – as Foster Associates did when their design team produced no less than 108 concept models for the later abandoned BBC Radio Centre project for Langham Place – is neither intellectual nor creative in the traditional fine-art sense. But the merits or otherwise of this computer-style number crunching are not at issue where technology transfer is concerned: the question here is whether the researching of alien technologies is a liberating force in the context of the Second Machine Age.

To find the nearest thing to a total acceptance of the priority of technology transfer in architecture today it is necessary to study the work of a former Foster associate, Richard Horden, the designer of a series of the purest technology transfer buildings yet constructed in Britain. Horden's 1984 Yacht House in Hampshire, and its successors embody all the principles of tech-nology transfer that have been sporadically applied by Norman Foster, but concentrated into the generating structural frame of a series of multi-purpose buildings. Horden finds his materials and methods in the high-performance components produced by the yacht spar and standing rigging industry. His unique 'wind frame' structural system is piggy-backed on the research and development capability – as well as the materials and methods – of the high-tech boat-building industry and its component suppliers. Horden's Yacht House alone shows, not only that architectural design developed from the central principle of multi-sourced industrial component combination is feas-ible, but that its results can even achieve a marginal cultural acceptability within a fine-art design tradition. With the Yacht House Horden has gone further than any living architect towards showing that a true architecture of technology transfer need be neither impoverished nor primitive.

Like Richard Horden, the London and Los Angeles practice of Future Systems Inc., with its partners Jan Kaplicky, David Nixon and Amanda Levete, whom we have met before in these pages, has striven for nearly ten years to develop an architecture of technology transfer. Future Systems has the distinction of being the only British firm of architects involved in the design of the 1996 NASA manned space station. The firm's projects, like the seminal projects of Archigram, lean clearly on technology transplanted from aerospace design, but they reach much further into the emulation of organic structures. Recently the deliberate presentation of their advanced structural system projects in the context of conventional architectural competitions, such as the

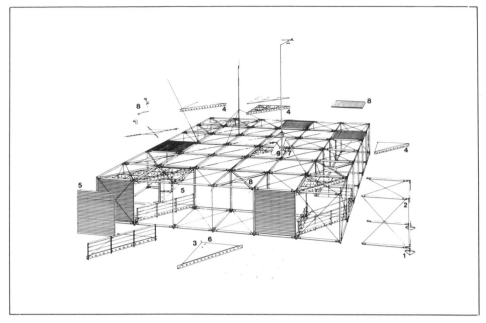

**105**   Yacht House by Richard Horden, 1984. Assembly drawing shows 'wind frame' of wire-braced Proctor yacht spars with fittings. *Key*: (1) Foundation baseplate. (2) 'Wind frame'. (3) Floor panel. (4) Roof panel. (5) Wall cladding. (6) Services. (7) Long span facility. (8) Canopies and screens (adapted from proprietary headsail reefing systems). (9) Accessories.

**106**   Yacht House by Richard Horden, 1984. A light, post-Miesian architecture of serendipitously chosen industrial products.

**107**  Future Systems: 'Peanut' house, 1983. Building encompassing articulated movement.

1985 Grand Buildings contest for Trafalgar Square, which Horden also entered, has begun to enable them to quantify the benefits of technology transfer in commercial terms. Working with a steel-framed semi-monocoque envelope built like the hull of a racing yacht, as well as self-cleaning ceramic external finishes derived from their NASA studies, their 'Gothic solution' Trafalgar Square project incorporating relocatable floors achieved a far higher net-to-gross ratio of usable floor area than any more orthodox competition entrant. The same powerful advantages were brought to bear on their premiated design for the 1989 Paris Bibliothèque Nationale competition.

It is only by such acts of stealth as Foster's carefully metered inclusions of alien technology within a fine-art-dominated culture, Future Systems' para-commercial designs, and Horden's unique yacht-mast structural system, that the architecture of technology transfer even remains visible under the obsolete Heritage value system that has ruled architecture since the end of the Modern mutiny. In reality, because it is a theory of architecture as multi-sourced element combination, technology transfer belongs to a different and more appropriate value system, alongside production engineering, automobile, marine and aerospace design, in the genetic pool of industrial systems combinations.

Eventually, Horden believes, the entire spectrum of manufactured components, from the smallest rigging screw to the largest offshore oil platform assembly, will become a hunting ground for transferable technology for building. He tends to draw elements for his designs from the smaller end of the component size continuum, but he sees the vast – as yet uncompiled – data base of all products as the proper area of search for the architect of the future.

But this revolution can never be achieved without the construction of a bridge from the present isolated world of stylistic façadism to this new conception of building as the product of cross-industry component and system combination. At present such a bridge can be built only upon the ability of architects like Foster, Horden, Whitehouse, Kaplicky and Nixon to live in both worlds, understanding the fertility of cross-industry specification, but still able to translate or 'culturalize' its results into the old fine-art value system. But such a double life is a compromise that imposes an enormous strain. Fortunately the blinkered attitude of the architectural profession is not found in all other areas of technology, and we could seek to apply a model from another sphere of human endeavour in which technology transfer was not only identified a long time ago, but an administrative structure to reinforce it is already sketched out.

In the United States the formation of the National Aeronautics and Space Administration in 1958 was followed in less than ten years by a report to the Congressional Committee on Science and Astronautics that not only noted numerous vital contributions to civilian technology that had been made by the transfer of defence-related techniques in the past,[16] but proposed the creation of a new class of professional personnel called 'transfer agents' whose responsibility would be solely to 'stimulate, accelerate and promote valid technology transfers through overt organized programmes'.

The words Charles Kimball, then president of the Midwest Research Institute, used in this Congressional Report of 1967 serve as well today as they did when they were written to define a kind of experimental prototype architect of tomorrow, who might serve the purposes of the built environment as well as the 'transfer agents' Kimball proposed to aid in the conquest of space.

'The type of person described here might be called an "applier of science" or, preferably, an "applier of technology",' Kimball wrote.

He (or she) will have two outstanding personal characteristics: an understanding of the world in which commercial forces operate, and a broad technical background . . . The time has come to consider carefully the deliberate development of techniques, university curricula, experiments and perhaps even new institutions to provide the nation with many more effective persons who can serve as 'appliers of technology' . . . These individuals need to be described, characterised, and identified as early as possible in their professional lives to provide them with significant and relevant educational opportunities, and then to provide working environments that will make their contribution meaningful. New technical ideas are transferred and implemented by persons – *not* by reports – and for persons to do this effectively, they must operate in an environment that is conducive to new-enterprise generation.[17]

The field of such a 'transfer agent' in architecture would be enormous. It might be defined as the positive of Richard Meier's negative description of the postmodern architect who 'ransacks the past, robs the present and obliterates the future'.[18] Architectural transfer agents would indeed ransack the past and rob the present, but it would be the entire past and present of technology that they would ransack, not one culturally defined fragment of it. Furthermore, far from obliterating the future, they would create new vistas for it. Kimball wrote 20 years ago that experience had shown him scientists and engineers made poor transfer agents: perhaps today architects would make better ones. Their first Congressional Report might become the first reference work of the architecture of the information age, a technological and methodological – rather than an art-historical – history of architecture.

Compared to the trivial works of style-history that presently crowd out genuine theory in the body of architectural knowledge, a serious analysis of technology transfer in buildings would have an immediate authority. It would unravel mysteries and explode myths with the clarity and force of such Modern pioneers as Adolf Loos or Le Corbusier. From the outset it would provide a much-needed objective base from which to compare the evolutionary and economic significance of pre-Modern, Modern and post-Modern architecture. Placed in the context of technology transfer, some post-Modern buildings, for example, might show themselves to be more fertile than their 'high-tech' counterparts. Terry Farrell's Clifton Nurseries building in Covent Garden, with its teflon-coated glass fibre roof membrane and its Proctor mast roof beams, is a case in point. And Classical Revival envelopes executed in profiled composite panels might be more impressive still, representing an ingenious way of 'culturalizing' the architectural use of such advanced boat-building composites as kevlar, epoxy and carbon fibre.

Clearly this new aesthetic of industrial *bricolage* requires design skills of a new order. But as in the case of the First Machine Age, by itself ability is not enough. The Modern pioneers could not have advanced as they did without the implicit support of steel and concrete industries eager for new markets, and neither can today's modest experiments in technology transfer grow into a new expertise in multi-sourced element combination without aid of the same kind. Most of all, technology transfer in architecture needs the help of robot-assembly industries like the motor industry that have already come to terms with incorporation of transferred technologies at all levels of design and production. In some ways the 'Gothic solution' commercial buildings described in chapter 5 already incorporate multi-sourced element combination in exactly the same way as the motor industry: steel frame from Britain, concrete from Greece, cladding from Germany, climate control equipment from the United States, work stations from Italy . . . It is only a step from the acknowledgement of this reality to 'percentages of local content' in buildings like those that operate successfully in the motor industry.

But all this is in the future. In contradistinction to the vast quantity of practically useless fine-art research that has been funded since architectural education abandoned pupillage and became an academic discipline,[19] the study of the transfer of materials and methods into building design from other fields has been neglected. Partial models for it may exist in studies of innovation in the construction industry that were carried out in the postwar years, notably those recorded in the United States by Burnham Kelly in *The Prefabrication of Houses* (1951), and in Britain by Marian Bowley's 1960 *Innovations in Building Materials* and her 1966 *The British Building Industry*, but that is all.

**108 (a)** and **(b)**    Terry Farrell, Clifton Nurseries, Covent Garden, 1982. Soon to be demolished, this structure showed the post-historical richness of technology transfer. Classical appearance (a) hides teflon-coated glass fibre fabric roof (b).

The tragedy of this absence is that, by setting aside the obfuscating camouflage of style, a deep study of the architecture of technology transfer would expose the massive material similarity that links all contemporary architecture – whatever its stylistic camouflage – and show more clearly than ever before what are the deep structures and what are the surface structures in the design of buildings. In this way the Byzantine world of contemporary architecture would suddenly become accessible to the quantitative analytical techniques that rule the late twentieth-century world of engineering design and manufacture.

Architecture, which is now nothing more than an occult world of ignorance and magic shot through with individual acts of achievement, could become a mega-technology. The mighty ocean of product information that can only presently be transferred as a result of fragmented, disorganized peripheral awareness, could be operationalized into a state of accessibility with the simplicity and directness of a video game. If an ideological certainty equal to that of the Modern Movement could be achieved for the new architecture of technology transfer, architects freed of the tyranny of history for the second time in a century could concentrate on design by assembly, identifying the availability of new materials and techniques, and if necessary 'specifying them into culture' with a squeeze on the joystick button. Like bees, architect transfer agents would be seen to have been carrying out an evolutionary as well as a productive task, their genetic role the cross-pollination of materials and methods from a whole earth catalogue of products into a one-world architecture of technology transfer.

## NOTES

1  It is in this sense that the term is used by Charles Kimball, in 1967 president of the Midwest Research Institute, in his paper 'Technology Transfer', published in *Applied Science and Technological Progress*, a report to the committee on science and astronautics of the US House of Representatives by the National Academy of Sciences, 1967.

2  The National Academy of Sciences report cites 11 major instances of technology transfer from defence to civilian applications alone between 1945 and 1967. These relate to matters such as computing, aero engine technology, air traffic control, glass fibre storage and pressure vessels, inorganic coatings, magnetic hammering, critical path and programme evaluation review, management techniques, and financial budgeting systems. The accelerometer example is perhaps the most unlikely.

3  A description of this building appears in the RIBA *Journal* for September 1983.

4  See 'Developments in the Structural Application of Light Gauge Galvanised Steel in Building', proceedings of a seminar organized by the Department of Civil Engineering of the University of Surrey, December 1979, Section 5.0, 'The Matrex Frame', by Nick Whitehouse.

5  I am indebted to Richard Horden for this example.

6  For an account of Reynolds's dome building technique see Martin Pawley, *Building for Tomorrow: Putting Waste to Work* (Sierra Club, San Francisco, 1982).

7  An account of the development of this 'plastic' armour is to be found in Gerald Pawle, *The Secret War* (Harrap, 1956). The Germans also made use of concrete armour up to 100 mm thick on *Sturmgeschutz IV* assault guns (see Eric Grove, *World War II Tanks*, Orbis, 1976). Years later Renzo Piano proposed a reinforced concrete platform chassis for a simple motor vehicle for developing countries.

8  Richard Buckminster Fuller, 'Designing a New Industry', an account of the development of the prefabricated WICHITA house, published as a pamphlet by the Fuller Research Institute, Wichita, Kansas in 1946; reprinted in *The Buckminster Fuller Reader*, ed. James Meller (Cape, 1970).

9  See Introduction, p. 7 above.

10  Banham, *Theory and Design*.

11  Donald Schon, *The Reflective Practitioner: How Professionals Think in Action* (Temple Smith, 1983).

12  Ayn Rand, *The Fountainhead* (Norton, 1943). See chapter 7, p. 167 below for a further discussion of this book.

13  The Peter Rice quotation is from a profile of the engineer published in *The Architects' Journal*, 21 and 28 December 1983.

14  The Michael Hopkins quotation is from *Building*, 8 November 1985.

15  Notably Norman Foster, who invariably cites instances of technology transfer when describing the design of such buildings as the Renault Centre (truck side-sheet tie-downs) or the Hongkong and Shanghai Bank (traditional Chinese bamboo scaffolding and motor industry-standard paintwork on the cladding), but refuses to grant the method primacy over fine-art considerations.

16  See note 2 above for a short list.

17  Kimball, National Academy of Sciences report, 1967.

18  A phrase used by the American architect Richard Meier in his RIBA Gold Medal acceptance speech in October 1988.

19  A decision taken at the Oxford Conference of 1958 that has contributed to the declining technical competence of architects in Britain ever since.

# CHAPTER 7

# Theory and Design in the Second Machine Age

> *There are meaningful warnings which history gives a threatened or*
> *perishing society. Such are, for instance, the decadence of art, or a lack of*
> *great statesmen. There are open and evident warnings too. The centre of*
> *your democracy and your culture is left without electric power for a few*
> *hours only, and all of a sudden crowds of citizens start looting and creating*
> *havoc. The smooth surface film must be very thin, the social system quite*
> *unstable and unhealthy.*
>
> ALEXANDER SOLZHENITSYN, 1978

THIS particular warning, which received Andy Warhol's statutory 15 minutes of fame in the United States but is now all but forgotten, has a formidable provenance. In Germany an entire philosophical tradition founded upon such warnings was erased after 1945, as a result of its association with the defeated forces of Fascism, and replaced by a form of logical positivism better attuned to the ideals of democratic social progress. But this assumption of rationality too proved impossible to reconcile with even a most utilitarian and practical industrial society. It was a misfit, perfectly illustrated by the grossly oversimplified philosophical insights of Robert Propst's *The Office: A Facility Based on Change*,[1] the effective bible of human performance in commerce for more than 20 years. So this positivism too gave way, this time to a more modest academic advocacy of 'communicative rationality' in the future. Alas, this was the Stalingrad of conformist philosophy, for from their already weakened position the rationalist school then went on to attack systems theory. Its thrust in the early 1970s ran head-on into linguistic studies and computer science, which had just begun their own clean sweep of all the outmoded 'searches for meaning' of philosophy. The result was the eclipse of 'communicative rationality' and the beginnings of a truly serviceable philosophy of global electronic awareness ruled by the blind advance of information science. From this new study of the medium instead of the message, by way of the elevation of electronic facts above human will, it was but a step to the acceptance of the rule of the machine, of power without objectives – and so once again to an endorsement of the irrational. In a nutshell, that is why today the rational Germans read the unread works of Klages and Spengler, Theodor Lessing and Carl Schmitt by osmosis, as it were, through the writings of the French post-Moderns.[2]

In England, apart from the impact of the translated works of the continental pioneers of Modernism, there has been no such philosophical odyssey. In fact there has been no philosophical input into design at all since the Arts and Crafts era of Ruskin and Morris. During the 1930s a shotgun marriage between this tradition and the theories of industrial design taught at the Bauhaus was hastily arranged by *émigré* art historians, and that was the end of the matter until the post-Modern revival of subjective irrationality began some 40 years later. Then, as in Germany and the United States, the consequence was the same abandonment of the *message* of social progress in favour of the *medium* of economic growth – or the assertion of the materiality of the significant over the metaphysics of the signified – as it is phrased in philosophical circles. In Germany the primary connection between philosophy, politics, planning and design survived even this trauma. In England it did not.

Throughout the twentieth century in England, design philosophy has been fictionalized. In architecture, as in morality and humour, fiction in the Anglo-Saxon world serves many purposes that would elsewhere be seen as philosophical. George Orwell's *Nineteen Eighty-four*, Aldous Huxley's *Brave New World*, and those few futuristic works of H. G. Wells that do not deter because of their taint of racism or imperialism, are the nearest to a genre of practical philosophy that the First Machine Age has to offer here. These novelists are our equivalents to Spengler, Heidegger, Sartre or Habermas. Their works are not ambitious philosophical treatises, but moral narratives, perhaps as significant in an academic sense as the novels of Albert Camus. The short story by Edward Morgan Forster (1879–1970) entitled 'The Machine Stops' is the most Solzhenitsyn-like of all of them.

'The Machine Stops' is a well-known premonition of technological doom. First published in 1911, and described by its author as 'a reaction to one of the earlier heavens of H. G. Wells', it tells the story of a subterranean technological society of the future in which (to use the depersonalized vocabulary of the present) declining technological skills lead to progressive systems failure and ultimate catastrophic disassembly. Surprisingly, in view of the early date of his writing, the author actually prefigures the physical form of a Fullerian world of capsule dwellings – 'small, hexagonal in shape like the cell of a bee' – in his imaginary underground settlements. But this foresight is weakened by his insistence on sowing the seeds of a happy ending for a heroic few, interestingly called 'the Homeless', and thus avoiding the total species extinction that is the essence of all philosophical – as opposed to fictional – visions of the end of the world as we know it.[3]

Forster was no Solzhenitsyn, although as novelists they are perhaps comparable. When Solzhenitsyn wrote of the Gulag and uttered his memorable jeremiads from exile in Vermont, of all the forbidden philosophical voices, the one he most resembled was that of Oswald Spengler (1880–1936) – who had been labouring over an immense catalogue of the rise and fall of civilizations when Forster dashed off his famous short story.

**109** Alexander Solzhenitsyn: looting and havoc are only just beneath the 'smooth surface film'.

**110** Edward Morgan Forster (1879–1970) as a young man: an ultimately romantic vision of the failure of the machine.

The first volume of Spengler's epic, *The Decline of the West*, was published in 1918, and the last in 1922. Ten years later he authorized the publication of a summary of the book based on lectures he had given, and this short version was called *Man and Technics*.[4] Spengler leapfrogged the bourgeois individualism that made Forster hypothesize outlaw survivors, and went on to adumbrate the coming of something very much like the irredeemable supermarket-looting urban underclass of Solzhenitsyn's late twentieth century. But he did repeat Forster's predicted mode of failure – his technological society too was brought to destruction, not by the failure of its life support machines, but by the degeneration of the technological intelligentsia in charge of them. As Thomas Mann wrote in a 1930 appreciation, what Spengler described was the threat to civilized life that arises when a culture has become incompetent, when it has ceased to honour its own scientific and technological prowess, has 'lived itself out, and its people have reverted to a primitive, unhistoried condition', becoming 'nomads of the big city' who are 'no longer the people, but formlessness, the end, nothingness'.[5]

Spengler was explicit about the role of discredited expertise in the collapse of machine civilization, but for him the collapse of architecture would merely have been a small part of it. In 1922, when Le Corbusier was drawing his first broad urban motorways lancing between rows of shining towers, Spengler was already predicting today's dying cities choked with motor traffic. He foresaw automation, unemployment, terrorism, sabotage, 'railways and steamships as dead as the Roman roads and the Chinese wall, our giant cities and skyscrapers in ruins like old Memphis and Babylon'.

In confronting this landscape of dereliction, Spengler saw it in the opposite way to Forster, not as an inevitable stage in a vast cycle of degeneration and renewal, but as a terminal barbarism into which mankind would sink forever if mastery of the universal and selfless service of machines were ever to be lost. Spengler saw the refusal to stand firm with technology as nothing less than a collective failure of human nerve, something that he felicitously termed 'conscientious objection in the battle with nature'. He saw in the yearnings of his time towards 'pure speculation, occultism, spiritualism and metaphysical inquisitiveness' something that he identified as moral cowardice. For him there was no 'Soft technology', or 'Green alternative'. He called upon the 'leaders of men' to force on the development of science in 'the clear cold atmosphere of technical organization' – a terminology that was to lead to his identification with the excesses of Nazi Germany, even though they occurred after his death. But apart from this association, it could be said that he gazed upon the same global technological society of the future as Richard Buckminster Fuller, albeit without the steadfast optimism that Fuller derived from his identification of the law of technological 'ephemeralization'. Spengler wrote: 'All great discoveries and inventions spring from the delight of strong men in victory. They are expressions of personality and not of the utilitarian thinking of the masses, who are merely spectators of the event, and must take its consequences whatever they may be.' Fuller believed that 'The effective decisions can only be made by independently thinking and adequately informed human individuals and their telepathically intercommunicated wisdom – the wisdom of the majority of all such human individuals.'[6]

Spengler ruled out any 'telepathically intercommunicated wisdom'. He believed in leadership and the responsibility of experts to rule through 'that mature and autumnal product, technical intellectuality'. Despite their differences, both Spengler and Fuller tried to identify a kind of Praetorian Guard or Samurai of modern technology, who would unwaveringly march ahead, undeterred by popular resentment, dire warnings or the siren call of the past. Spengler saw these men (for, characteristically of his time, he did not imagine the task might fall to women), not as team workers engaged in some vast cooperative enterprise – as Fuller liked to see the global participants in his grandiloquent 'World Design Science Decade' of the 1960s – but as individual men of genius and power. Spengler's engineers were not placemen, politicians or intriguers, passing resolutions, deliberating on boards, in parliaments or in palaces: they had the overt authority and responsibility of generals.

For Spengler, the creation of nineteenth-century machine civilization had been an imperial task, comparable to but greater than the building of the civilizations of Greece and Rome; 'a grand technical development only made possible because the intellectual level (of engineers, organizers and discoverers) was constantly becoming higher'. So wonderfully efficient had been the machine civilization created by these men that by the dawn of the twentieth century the global continuation of their work required no more than 'a hundred thousand outstanding brains'. It was the sole duty of this technological elite, Spengler insisted, to sustain and enlarge the great edifice.

But, unlike their forefathers, this successor generation confronted a new enemy. Within their own class there was a growing indifference and waywardness, and beyond it an outright 'mutiny of the mass of the people against their destiny, against the machine, against organized life, against anything and everything'. This mutiny was the uprising of the mob identified 50 years later by Solzhenitsyn, in the form of 'sudden crowds of citizens looting and creating havoc', waiting only for a brief failure in the electricity supply to rupture 'the thin smooth surface film' of an unstable social system.

Because of what he perceived as the extreme vulnerability of the machine, Spengler dwelt on the crucial influence of this renegade elite, the 'conscientious objectors in the war against nature'. These persons, the 'Greens' of our day, were the reason that he went beyond Forsterian failure in his vision of the future, although not perhaps with the full inevitability that the title of his book suggests. He exhorted the creative, managerial and engineering elite to do its duty, and held up the example of the rise and fall of previous civilizations to encourage them, but he prepared them also for the ultimate sacrifice. Unlike Fuller's 'design scientists' of half a century later who, like Scientologists, were instructed that the terms 'success' and 'failure' and 'good' and 'bad' are all meaningless, Spengler's elite leaned on a military conception of victory or defeat. Whether or not the rebellion of the conscientious objectors was overcome, his technological Samurai would stand by their machines. If the worst should come to the worst . . . 'We are born into this time and must bravely follow its path to the destined end,' he wrote. 'Only dreamers believe there is a way out. Optimism is cowardice.'

It is in his exaltation of an earlier technocratic elite that Spengler is most instructive to the reader of 70 years later. Like an astronomer convinced that the earth is the only inhabited planet in the universe, Spengler constantly stressed the vulnerability and uniqueness of the First Machine Age. 'To invent these wheels and set them working . . . that is something which only a few *born* thereto can achieve . . . These must be creative talents, enthusiasts for their work, and formed for it by a steeling of years' duration at great expense,' he wrote. The *born* technological leaders who rise from his pages are archetypes, if not architects, models for a modern ideal that was perplexingly destined to flower under positivism rather than metaphysics.

In *The Decline of the West* Spengler unconsciously wrote a job description for the pioneers of Modern architecture, and in the 50 years that followed its publication, they fulfilled it to the letter. From where else came Frank Lloyd Wright's concept of architecture as 'Truth against the world', Mies van der

Rohe's conviction that 'the individual is losing significance and his destiny is no longer what interests us', or Le Corbusier's vision of the mass production of buildings as a means whereby 'Je ferai des maisons comme on fait des voitures'? All of these visions and more came from this one world view. Tellingly, Spengler's imperious technological man is the prototype too of Ayn Rand's 1943 fictional Modern architect, Howard Roark, the hero and genius of *The Fountainhead* so lovingly reinvoked in Andrew Saint's *The Image of the Architect*, where Roark's famous courtroom defence echoes the words of Spengler to the letter: 'No work is ever done collectively by a majority decision. Every creative job is achieved under the guidance of a single individual thought. An architect requires a great many men to erect his building. But he does not ask them to vote on his design.'[7]

Today these inflexible men of genius are out of fashion, but not more so than the prophet who sang their praises. Against the legend of the great Modern pioneers is ranged an entire armoury of arguments denouncing the cult of personality in the twentieth century. Saint as usual is apposite in his choice of quotations, this time from the architect-author of a messianic volume entitled *Architecture by Team*[8] who wrote in 1971:

Not long ago I read a newspaper account of the opening of a public building in which the architect was given quite a spread. If quoted correctly, within two short paragraphs the architect said, 'I did this' or 'I did that' six times, and 'my building' twice. Yet did he really do the building? Didn't he get just a little help? Did he draw every line? Make every engineering calculation? Specify the cement, aggregate, and texture of concrete? Estimate the cost?[9]

**111** Oswald Spengler (1880–1936) warned against 'conscientious objection in the battle with nature'.

167

Our commercial architect-author may do little more than paraphrase Brecht – although he is almost certainly unconscious of it – but he exposes the enlargement that 50 years had already brought to the popular revolt that Spengler had prepared his Samurai to resist to the death. It is not technology that is wrong, say the 'conscientious objectors' now, but directing its application and then claiming the credit – in fact the very concept of individual 'victory' that lay at the heart of invention and achievement in Spengler's machine civilization. Irrationally – as though the two could be separated – the rebels called for the authority of the engineers, architects, artists and technicians to be curbed, but not their expertise. In the words of Prince Charles, the most illustrious of all the 'conscientious objectors',

For far too long architects have consistently ignored the feelings and wishes of the mass of ordinary people in this country . . . architects and planners do not necessarily have the monopoly of knowing best about taste, style and planning . . . ordinary people should not be made to feel guilty or ignorant if their natural preference is for more traditional designs.[10]

And not just architects and planners. Four years later the same Prince dismayed an audience of dignitaries at the opening of a 'Museum of the Moving Image' in London by exploding in virtually the same words:

It is palpable nonsense to say that violence on TV has no effect on people's behaviour! The people who say this are so-called experts who attempt to confuse ordinary people so they feel they do not know what they are talking about!

**112** HRH Prince Charles. Acting out 'conscientious objection' on the part of the man in the street.

Clearly the central question is not whether 'so-called experts' have the ability to mind the machines of the machine age, even if their technical competence is occasionally challenged. The question now is: Upon what terms shall they be allowed to continue to mind them? If they insist upon methods that 'confuse ordinary people', perhaps they should be swept away, like the recalcitrant air traffic controllers of the United States – 11,000 of whom were dismissed after they took industrial action in 1981, only to be replaced by newly trained substitutes within two years.

The episode of the air traffic controllers has attracted too little attention. It proved that the complete replacement of a very specialized expertise was possible, or at least it seemed so to those who feel no terror at the thought of losing expertise – as though it were a species like the whale – forever. To such stout hearts it is far more important not to be bamboozled into thinking that they don't know what they are talking about, for it is what they think that counts. They think that the complexity of science and technology is a conspiracy; that any fool can get oil out of the ground or from the seabed; that any blacksmith can knock up a windmill to make electricity; and anybody, anybody at all, can design all the buildings we will ever need.

The 'conscientious objectors' who hold these opinions have in mind new role models for a replacement cadre of machine minders. They can be 'consultants', 'power sharers', 'community architects', 'self-builders', 'technical aid persons', or professional public opinion samplers in the employ of benign multinational corporations – all of whom are preferable to today's 'so-called experts' who make 'ordinary people feel guilty'. In any case there are already many such new-style technopersons in existence: 'team players' who do not require 'victory' (or even know what it is) and are so well satisfied with the endorsement of their projects by public opinion rather than the opinion of their peers that they might even *demand* a vote on all their designs. Such individuals will gratefully navigate a received world of permissions, presentations, grants and applications. They like to fill out forms, 'negotiate', 'participate', 'compromise', 'guarantee' and 'insure'. They are happy to share responsibility, happier still to unload it altogether.

To an alarming extent these new-style politicians of the environment are the architects and engineers of the Second Machine Age. For them design is a 'situation', not a duty, and where conflicts arise they take the side of Spengler's 'mass of executive hands' – the only side, as he wrote, 'that discontent will look upon'. These new figures are of the elite by name, but they lack the authority by which elites were recognized in the past, and they refuse to play by the old professional rules. Instead they act out Spengler's 'flight of the born leader from the machine', 'conscientiously objecting' to the battle between technology and nature. Spengler identified them in advance as the most dangerous of all the enemies of science and technology, persons whose deceptively modest plea is for the Second Machine Age to be slowed down or suspended on full pay pending an inquiry. He was not impressed. As he contemptuously observed, 'Even a sheep could bring that about, if it were to fall into the machinery.'

Spengler's vision here is at its most acute. Although he died more than 50 years ago he could hardly have better characterized the architects and designers of the twentieth century, men and women who, with the aid of contemporary equivalents of 'pure speculation, occultism, spiritualism or metaphysical inquisitiveness' – such as 'Conceptual Architecture', 'Conservation', 'Deconstruction', 'Classical Revival', 'Postmodernism' or 'Community Architecture' – do indeed reject their stern technological duty in favour of one Bundalog nostrum after another. Instead of focusing upon the gigantic environmental problems massing upon the horizon, they pursue the chimera of the image cascade, the fickle endorsement of 'the masses, who are merely spectators of the event, and must take its consequences whatever they may be'.[11]

This new generation rejects the overt respect that expert status automatically drew from earlier generations; it calls instead for the politicization of its own leadership and speaks of a power reversal – 'from the bottom up' – a bizarre contradiction in terms repeatedly endorsed by the Prince of Wales in his periodic effusions of enthusiasm for the kitsch of the housing market that he mistakes for architecture.

The consequence of this orgy of bad faith and self-deception is inevitable. Where there is no philosophy but only fiction, there can be no elucidation but only termination. When the leaders of this army of 'conscientious objectors' finally do summon up the courage to address their own shameful refusal to pick up their new tools, master their fast-evolving new technology, and start to put right what was wrong before . . . they present it as a triumph!

The way in which they do this is extraordinary. Into the dustbin of history goes the grand performance of leadership and obedience that was Modernism; on to the stage of the environment, to be greeted by a roar from the crowd, steps defeat snatched from the jaws of victory. The era of vast plans that could be made and carried out in the broad light of day is over – and good riddance! So too are the days of technical problems that could be publicly explained and publicly tackled; evils that could be universally acknowledged, analysed and eradicated; even futures that could be foreseen without dread. Goodbye to all that! In its place, blinking in the glare of spotlights, we see the new men, shallow men disguised in identical business suits. In unison they speak the words of Lionel Esher, the weakest Modern spirit of all: 'A change of consciousness is at work in the world, a change as profound as the one we associate with the Renaissance, but almost its mirror image. In this view the retreat from heroic plans, from mass solutions and from self-indulgent architecture, like other British retreats, is not a defeat but a victory.'[12]

And what is the name of this 'victory'? It is the new myth, the myth of a Dunkirk of the built environment, through which an army all but lost to arrogance was saved by a fleet of little ships (the people themselves, who refuse any longer to be 'confused' or 'made to feel guilty or ignorant'). This myth pervades the architecture of the Second Machine Age, for the Americans too have their version of the defeat-that-was-a-victory, that casts Modernism as a 'learning experience' from which its practitioners can be 'born again', baptized by total immersion in ornament. The myth says that this image-changing rite can enable the architect to retain all his privileges, even as he sheds his old responsibilities, by streaking through history.

According to this view the Spenglerian image of the architect of the First Machine Age as an 'arrogant' technocratic 'expert' must be replaced by another and newer image of the architect appropriate to the energized, ephemeralized, nothing-is-what-it-seems postmodern world. This new image is of a magician, modest but tireless, always prepared to ask for advice, always eager to learn, always ready to revise his drawings, always reluctant to stand his ground, always ready to try again. This is the 'enabler', not the 'provider', the younger, harder-working, more flexible, less principled architect-politician of the façade and the 'elevational treatment' whose work we increasingly see around us today. How up-to-date he is, with an office like NASA Mission Control and a car stuffed with as much communications technology as a mobile divisional headquarters! And yet how perfectly his real role and his crippling limitations were identified by Forster, Spengler and Fuller, at least 50 years ago. Let Forster speak for all of them:

No one confessed the Machine was out of hand. Year by year it was served with increased efficiency and decreased intelligence. The better a man knew his own duties upon it, the less he understood the duties of his neighbour, and in the world there was not one who understood the monster as a whole. Those master brains had perished.[13]

The master brains of the First Machine Age did perish. In architecture far more than engineering or management, the loss was irreparable. The most important and only indisputable fact about architecture in the age of science was that science overtook it and, politeness aside, the overtaking occurred for reasons to which Forster, Spengler and Fuller are better guides than Reyner Banham or Charles Jencks. The Dunkirk myth of postmodernism is only a myth. There never was a professional rebellion against 'a dehumanized technological environment'; no 'change as profound as the one we associate with the Renaissance'. All that happened was that the Keynesian economy collapsed and the sons of the oligarchy of Modernism suffered a loss of nerve. When the great public spending boom of the postwar period ended, when in the fullness of time the great actors died – Wright, Mies van der Rohe, Gropius, Le Corbusier – there were no competent followers. Modern architecture had misunderstood its relationship with technology, adjusted itself too well to a Keynesian war economy, and failed to reproduce. Like the monarchies that had so often been its clients in history, architecture suffered a succession crisis. From the strong generation of 1914, who seized the initiative, mastered the technology and convinced the world – the mantle of authority descended to the weak generation of 1968, who lost the initiative, couldn't keep up with the technology, and believed the world too much.

Neither their loss of conviction, nor their innocent fumbling with authority, nor their deliberate confusion of duty with popularity, nor their dismal loss of nerve in the face of mounting complexities prevented the new generation from mounting the thrones that one by one were vacated. But their most crucial failure, the inability to grasp that proud professional competence and the ability to enforce it were the most vital asset of all, guaranteed disaster. The passage of time brought into positions, that were once seats of power and influence, pygmies who were not what their credentials proclaimed. The once marvellous 'technical intellectuality' created by the giants of the First Machine Age was handed down to planners who made no plans, architects who designed no buildings, historians who knew no history, critics who praised distinctions without differences.

The first crushing blows came with the recession of the 1970s, and not with the never-had-it-so-good easy living of the 1960s – when the transfer of power from the giants to the pygmies had silently occurred. One blow was the collapse of public sector spending and the withdrawal of social architecture from the political agenda. Another was the massive and long-foretold impact of electronic communications on the great cities, and its creation of an embryonic alternative environment of informationalized dispersed development. Another was the grim certainty that, because there was no mastery of new materials and methods, and because building procurement was tied down by a scarcity value system and an ancient and unchanged subservience to property rights, the rate of reproduction of buildings would never be high enough to enable their design to catch up with the need for 'serviced situations' that Kaufmann – so accurately foresaw 25 years ago.[14]

Because of this obsolescence at the heart of the building process, all new building – with the possible exception of the fastest interior refurbishments of existing structures – may already be out of date. Notwithstanding epic performances in contract management, the only practical economic difference between new buildings and the seething, undifferentiated mass of 'Heritage' structures they replace may be that they cost more money and take longer to bring on stream.

The result has been an ever-increasing number of construction professionals, each with an exponentially increasing capacity for work (because of new computer-aided design and drafting technology), but a more and more closely circumscribed arena in which to operate. In this shrinking perimeter lie the hulks of all the great techno-professions – like the separate armed forces, army, navy, and air force – of 30 years ago.

As the territory available to each diminishes, these professions will colonize and merge, leaving empty academic superstructures behind. In the end, in a final emulation of the agglomeration achieved by the motor industry half a century ago, there will be only a single, integrated construction profession consisting of a dozen high-technology multi-disciplinary firms – probably all of which already exist – that will be capable of handling every aspect of building procurement.

Side by side with the formation of this new corporate oligarchy, public dissatisfaction at the mismatch between the scale of the environmental crisis and the performance of the forces brought to bear on it will grow. And its anger will turn from the still independent building professions to all the 'special task forces', 'urban renewal agencies', and 'development corporations' thrown into the battle by beleaguered politicians. Notwithstanding this plethora of new job descriptions, the professional leaders of a construction industry that for decades has ploughed a bare 0·5 per cent of its turnover into research and development – as opposed to 18 per cent in electronics and aerospace – will be unable to satisfy the masses whose hopes it so unwisely triggered by its unrestrained criticism of the recent past. The demands of commercial building users will finally force a general recognition of the fact that finite, fine-art, architecture no longer describes any recognizable urban reality. At this point the philosophy of continuous change and rapid building obsolescence, against which the architectural profession has fought for more than 50 years, will flood through the popular consciousness. And when this development is finally recognized, there will be almost no architectural ideology left into which it can be made to fit. A new language of ceaseless urban movement will have to be adopted and art history will finally be capped off like an empty oil well. Architecture, its history, its supposed importance and all the arguments about it, will become just one part of what is vulgarly known as 'a turnkey operation'; and Spengler's need for one hundred thousand first-class brains will shrink to only one thousand.

Survival for individual architects in this new landscape will become increasingly a matter of searching for the folds and creases in the Fullerian world map to find out what shape it is finally going to compress itself into. Architects today are already spread dangerously thin over a miraculously vast territory in the popular consciousness – 'Architects? They design buildings don't they?' Do they indeed! Massive development conglomerates on the one hand, and massive regulatory bureaucracies on the other will be the two poles of architecture in the twenty-first century – and most independent architects will vanish as rapidly into their corporate grasp as did the once equally numerous and loquacious independent estate agents who recently disappeared, unlamented, into the maw of the banks and building societies.[15]

Between the giants of the future there will still of course be solo freelance operators, enjoying the same relationship with the assembled subcontractors of construction as software writers do with the giants of the computer industry today. These individuals, counterparts perhaps to Forster's 'Homeless' who inherit the earth, will have all the freedom of the old-style independent professional, but none of his authority. They may use the name 'architect', but when they work it will be as clerks, with the humiliating privilege of rubber-stamping compliance with vernacular aesthetic prejudice, or as designers who, even if they fight their way into the image cascade, will have no alternative but to be absorbed into the mechanism of the giants.

More important by far than the fate of the professionals is the fact that all this reconfiguration is already taking place against the background of an intractable and worsening crisis in the real environment. Today, even at record levels of output, less than one half of one per cent of the built environment can be replaced in a single year – as opposed to 12 per cent of the population of motor vehicles. And the restrictions imposed by Buckminster Fuller's 'money making' economy ensure that 'record levels' of building, in the sense understood by the Victorians, the Modern pioneers of prefabrication, or any truly 'ephemeralized' industry today, are not even on the agenda. It was to this real crisis, and not the problems of popularity, that the technological Samurai should have addressed themselves, and it is to the consequences of their failure to do so that we must now turn.

Ten years off the turn of the century, London offers a perfect example of *The Decline of the West*, and a lesson that is fraught with serious consequences for all industrial societies. Even as its massive new satellite-communication developments of London Wall, London Bridge City, Canary Wharf and King's Cross crawl towards completion, 124-mile traffic jams between London and Bristol and complete stoppages on the M25 motorway become a repeating occurrence. Two new railheads and two new motorways are lancing across northern France towards three pitifully narrow tubes that will link them beneath the Channel to an ancient railway network and an inadequate motorways system on the British side.[16] Beyond this jumble the city lies inert behind its barrage of fine-art and conservationist propaganda. A vast junkpile of all the building materials of history, its intellectual infrastructure is scarcely less vital than its physical form. As we have briefly mentioned before, proposals to punch beneath this vast sprawl of impenetrable built entanglements with tunnelled roadways and subterranean parking garages are fought off with academic 'theories' that scarcely deserve the name. 'Building more roads will mean more cars and more congestion' is the unhelpful verdict of a London University professor who allegedly specializes in transport studies.[17] Meanwhile the congested city sets more and more into the pattern of life of the trenches in the Great War: a life of movable but unremovable obstructions through which even motor cycle dispatch riders can move no faster than foot soldiers through mud and machine gun fire.

In the true sense that Spengler predicted, no one is in control of this city – although many have titles that imply that they have responsibility for it.[18] As far as physical planning and building are concerned it is already too late to do anything about London that will have any measurable effect within any politically useful timescale. No responsible person in architecture, planning or politics any longer believes either that planning in the manner of the Ville Radieuse or Broadacre City is the answer, or that the guiding intelligence,

113 The City of London during the Blitz in 1941. Like Broadgate under construction.

executive power and popular obedience exist anywhere within the body politic to make it happen. In that sense it is already terrifyingly obsolete.

The fate of architecture diminishes in the colossal shadow of this battle between the future operations of the economy and the intransigent obstruction of a city that is now the sum of all the discarded options of its past. As Spengler believed, a state of war does exist, but not only between man and nature; between the age of science and the accumulated infrastructure of centuries as well. To say that planning is impossible in modern conditions – and this is often said – is itself virtually an admission of the existence of this state of war. In war you take things as you find them and do the best you can to get through – which is what information technology (the new philosophy) already does with the intractable architecture of the past. The economy of the city today requires its citizens to fight: they fight its obstructive physical structure and overloaded systems as though it were a vast wasteland of natural or man-made obstacles.

Any such 'solid state' or post-Modern city (which is to say any world city that has ceased to think in terms of managing its own growth, ceased to control its intake of citizens, ceased to be able to identify, let alone assert civic interests over commercial demand) that city, be it London, Cairo, Mexico City, Los Angeles or Tokyo, is already at war, and the term is hardly any longer figurative. London is astonishingly similar today to the London of the World War Two Blitz. So dense is its traffic and so great the volume of its construction in progress that any attempt to cross its centre forces to mind the 1940 description by J. M. Richards, who wrote of 'that peculiar air-raid smell of wet charred wood, and the blundering gait with which we picked our way over puddled streets crisscrossed with hoses'.[19]

It is as the war zone that it is today, not the conservationist paradise of new yesterday, or the utopian paradise of old tomorrow, that we must learn to look at the city in order to understand the failure of theory and design in the Second Machine Age. This city is not planned or designed, it is chaotic and out of control: its streets are like trenches; its traffic is armour; its forest of signs are military rendezvous points. Its street life is like life in no man's land. Its crime is combat. Its drugs are chemical weapons. Its policemen are military policemen.

All the major redevelopment projects of this city, the immense commercial developments that boggle the minds of property correspondents, stir the anxieties of the trimmers of the Royal Fine Art Commission, drive in the pickets of the voluntary conservation organizations and alert the great mother ship, English Heritage, all these projects have two faces. In one way they are simply proposals for millions of square feet of serviced floorspace, scheduled to be available in three, five or seven years' time: in another they are solemn promises of urban disruption for three, five or seven years ahead. Taking the second way first, we can see these monsters – Broadgate, London Bridge City, Canary Wharf, London Wall – as bids in a galactic game of roulette. Each bid may not be a winner, but it is a guarantee of uncertainty and a long period of obstruction, inconvenience, pollution and incidental environmental damage.

**114**  Broadgate under construction, 1986. Not totally dissimilar to the Blitz.

Take a dozen of these big bids whirling at once on the vast money wheel of any city centre and you have the third way of looking at the city; as a heaving, slow-motion battleground. Take three dozen of these bids, staggered in time, and you have 70 years of built-in obsolescence; a lifetime lived in the shadow of destruction and reconstruction with the hope of a finished, perfect city of the future perpetually deferred. Architecture, whatever its surface style, is not important in this slow-motion battle: it is not part of the answer, it is part of the problem.

The role of information technology in this urban wargame of the Second Machine Age is exactly the same as its role in any war – it compensates for the impenetrability of the war zone that the built environment has become, and thus drives fear of it from our consciousness. One of the most instructive things about signs, images and all electronic media is the way in which they effortlessly keep pace with this slide into environmental war. In part this is because information technology originated as military technology – the telephone-equipped four-wheel-drive company car is only a civilian version of the World War Two mobile command headquarters; in part too it is because the indirect geography and unpredictable constructions of the erupting city have made our dependence upon information in the urban environment complete. We are lost in the metropolis without information. In the urban war, as in any war, we know only what we are told. If a war zone is where thought is impossible, then thought must be supplied from outside, by information.

What this means is that the real city of the Second Machine Age – the city perceived in our consciousness – is a binary phenomenon. One part of our brain knows that the information part of the city is *assembling*, despite all this physical chaos and congestion. It is slowly knitting itself together like a vast computer image behind which is a stupendous octopus of electronic awareness whose head is a satellite in outer space and whose tentacles reach into and between all other cities everywhere. At the same time the other part of our brain knows that the physical city of immobile architecture is *disassembling*, becoming a semiologically homogenized warren of temporary façades, fronting on to free fire zones populated by muggers, clampers, beggars and the paralysed armoured divisions of traffic locked in their deadly embrace.

Put together, these two images create a stereoscopic picture in which what was once the public realm, the civic vistas and spaces, the now clogged and useless streets and the crime-prone squares and parks of the city have been engulfed by the war zone and converted into an exhausting topography of obstructions. At the same time the inner information world, including the media, is busy miniaturizing the job that all that public space used to do. Part of the crisis of architecture in the Second Machine Age is that it must learn to face the fact that information does not need the public realm – which was the progenitor of historic architecture. Until it learns that lesson it will have no more real significance than a man-made range of mountains.

It is popular nowadays to speculate on the possibility of the electronic octopus of information 'breaking the stalemate' of the urban war by leaping over the physical barriers of streets and buildings – just as the primitive tanks of 1916 were supposed to enable the army to break out of the deadlock of trench warfare. This can happen, indeed it already has, but as the task of information ceases to be to direct the war of urban development but to evade it instead, the new configuration reveals itself to be 'dispersal' – another uncanny repetition of military practice. In the United States for example, at General Motors' Vanguard plant in Saginaw, there is a perfect parody of a World War Two 'shadow factory'. As a motor magazine enthusiastically reports, 'The only workers apart from a handful of maintenance men and systems managers, are robots working in "cells" connected by scuttling wire-guided trolleys. Raw components go in at one end, complete front-drive half shaft assemblies emerge from the other.' In an unconscious parody of the wartime blackout, 'Vanguard will soon operate "lights out" for its night shift.'[20]

Such dispersal does not put an end to the urban war even if it does break free of the deadlock of the urban trenches. It converts it instead into a war of movement. And under these conditions the military operations of the economy – raging like a blitzkrieg unchecked by the discredited defence of decayed and corrupt local planning legislation – turn out to demand an appropriately revolutionary transformation in the use of land such as 'prairie farming' over large areas, light industry and commerce dispersed along 'motorway corridors', the blurring of the distinction between the urban and the rural workforce. Notwithstanding political differences, parallels to all of these can be found in the Soviet Five Year Plans of the First Machine Age. As Berthold Lubetkin wrote in 1932,

Through the disurbanisation of towns and the urbanisation of the country we shall achieve an abolition of the contradictions between the urban and the agricultural proletariat. We must not have concentrated and unhealthy habitations but throughout the country endless streams of human dwellings along the big arteries of contemporary life joining our centres of industry and agriculture. Existing towns are doomed to quick extinction, only the art monuments must remain, surrounded by vast parks.[21]

This too is a battle plan, a plan for an environmental war that is as endless as Oswald Spengler claimed, so endless in fact that, incredible as it may seem, we can set Josef Stalin's collectivization programme of sixty years ago beside the 'enterprise culture' of Margaret Thatcher's Britain – and the join is invisible.

Of course all the possibilities of architecture in the Second Machine Age are not subsumed by its paralysis in the war zone of the city. But it is in the urban crisis that its failure can be most clearly seen today by those with the courage to face things as they really are. The urban war may be but one front of the environmental war of the Second Machine Age, but it is one front of a total war, like all the wars of the twentieth century. This time the protagonists are not nation states or alliances, but the power of the science and technology created by our species on one side, and the accumulated infrastructure and waste of our own history on the other.

The Second Machine Age began with the awareness of the power of information and the birth of cybernetic control. At the end of it all human beings, formerly protagonists in the schemes of conquest and rule that we call civilizations and cultures, have been left in a state of unprecedented redundancy. Philosophically we confront the most radical position of all, which is to accept that there are forces of organization far beyond our control that have removed the initiative from the hands of the human creators and the protectors of the built environment. These are instantaneous, inexhaustible forces of energy, communication and production that have no territorial goals or objectives. They are inanimate but invincible; they are intelligent but they

have no ideas; they lack ambition but they conquer all; they need neither leaders nor followers. They are objects that need no subject. Moral interventions, value judgements, saying that this is good or that is bad – all of that merely disrupts the process by which they are assembling the future. The search for meaning, the protection of the past, individual creativity, the proof of being right – all that is now merely a needless risk.[22]

In the Second Machine Age our society has become so vulnerable in its dependence on these forces, so hard-wired in its reliance on their goalless energy, that expecting the unexpected from the exercise of individual genius borders on naivety. The most radical thing that any of us can do now is to do nothing, to wait while the instantaneous forces of the Second Machine Age work out how to construct a future upon the relics of the past that we no longer have the will or the authority to change. In this vacuum, those architects who are content to remain 'conscientious objectors in the battle with nature' may find their time is running out.

# NOTES

1 Robert Propst, *The Office: A Facility Based on Change* (Herman Miller, 1968). Readers may be surprised to see this tract on space planning and office furniture under the heading of philosophy, but the book has been in print for more than 20 years and no volume better illustrates the application of logical positivist thought to design, and the hopelessly limited conception of human personality and motivation that accompanies it.

2 This account of the fascinating journey of German philosophy from irrationality and metaphysics, through logical positivism, communicative rationality and systems theory back to irrational postmodernism is taken from Manfred Frank ('Contemporary German Philosophy', *Kultur Chronik*, 5/1988). The reference to the 'forbidden' German origin of much French postmodernist thought comes from an essay by Jaques Bouveresse entitled 'Spengler's Revenge', and from remarks by Derrida at the 1986 *Rencontres Franco–Germaniques* in Paris.

3 E. M. Forster, 'The Machine Stops', first published in the anthology *The Celestial Omnibus* in 1911. Although Forster's underground civilization of the future suffers progressive equipment failure, there are outlaw survivors contriving to live on the surface of the planet even after the catastrophe. In this sense 'The Machine Stops' is in a humanist tradition quite unlike such postwar works of prophecy as Herman Kahn's *On Thermonuclear War* (Greenwood Press, 1978), or Gordon Rattray-Taylor's *The Doomsday Book* (Thames & Hudson, 1970).

4 Oswald Spengler, *The Decline of the West* (2 vols), translated by Charles Francis Atkinson, was published by Alfred Knopf, 1932 and 1963. *Man and Technics*, based on a series of lectures Spengler delivered in 1931, was also translated by Charles Francis Atkinson and published by Knopf in 1932 and 1963. The quotations here are all from the 1963 edition of *Man and Technics*.

5 Thomas Mann, *Past Masters* (Martin Secker, 1933), a collection of writings

**115** OPPOSITE 'The search for meaning, individual creativity . . . all that is now merely a needless risk.' Chernobyl from the air, 1986.

including the essay 'On the Theory of Spengler'. Mann is interesting as a pre-1945 anti-Fascist supporter of Spengler's world view.

6 Richard Buckminster Fuller, *Critical Path* (Hutchinson, 1983). This was the last book Fuller published in his lifetime, nearly 50 years after Spengler died.

7 Ayn Rand, *The Fountainhead* (Norton, 1943). As Andrew Saint (*The Image of the Architect*, Yale, 1983) points out with his admirable summary of the plot, this novel is still in print and has sold over five million copies and 'could hardly have sold as it has done without some popular willingness to confirm and indulge Ayn Rand's ideal of the architectural profession'. In other words it is at least partly true.

8 William Wayne Caudill, *Architecture by Team* (Van Nostrand Reinhold, 1971).

9 Prince Charles, 'People should not be made to feel guilty . . .' From a speech delivered on 30 May 1984 to the Royal Institute of British Architects at Hampton Court on the occasion of the award of the Royal Gold Medal for Architecture to the Indian architect Charles Correa.

10 Prince Charles, 'So-called experts . . .'. From a speech delivered at the opening of the Museum of the Moving Image in London. Report in *The Times*, 16 September 1988.

11 Spengler, *Man and Technics*.

12 Lionel Esher, *The Broken Wave: The Rebuilding of Britain 1945–1970* (Allen Lane, 1981). As a protagonist in the postwar Modern triumph Esher is perverse in finding his Renaissance outside, rather than inside, the greatest architectural phenomenon of the century.

13 Forster, 'The Machine Stops'.

14 Edgar Kaufmann Jr., 'Design sans peur et sans ressources', *Architectural Forum*, September 1966. See also chapter 5, pp. 123–4.

15 The unreal status of the architectural profession today was acknowledged by the promoters of the 'Campaign for Architects', a promotional scheme launched by several practices with the aid of a major advertising agency in 1989. Not only did the campaign repeat a 1987 London and Westminster poll that showed 41 per cent of potential clients were aware that other professionals, chiefly surveyors, could offer the same service as architects, but a founding member, David Rock, of architects Rock Townsend, was quoted as saying: 'We must take advantage of the widely publicised belief, *whether it be right or not*, that it is architects who are responsible for the design of buildings and the environment' (italics supplied).

16 Had the planning giants of the First Machine Age been heeded in the Second Machine Age, all this might have been avoided. Sir Patrick Abercrombie's far-sighted 1944 *Plan for London* called for no less than five orbital motorways, but even a reduced version of this strategy was fought to a standstill by 'conscientious objectors' in the 1960s.

17 Dr Martin Mogridge, Transport Studies Group, University College, London, reported in *The Times*, 8 December 1988.

18 As we have noted earlier, the term 'plan' itself has fallen into disrepute in the enterprise culture, even as the Metropolitan planning authorities have been disbanded. In London's Docklands the word 'framework' is actually used instead of the term 'planning'. Major landscape gardening practices, like Gillespies, Clouston and Lovejoy, now undertake this 'framework' preparation – whose physical results in the form of drawings are indistinguishable from 'plans' – for development corporations and local authorities, but without the powers that formerly went with the title of 'planner'.

Interestingly the then president of the Royal Town Planning Institute, John Anderson, himself described the new limits of planning at a conference on development control in 1984. He argued that henceforth 'dictatorship by the planning authority' should be avoided. 'Planning,' he said, 'should be more like running a design school than issuing a blueprint' (R T P I press release, 6 April 1984). This freewheeling notion can be contrasted with the view of any Modern planning pioneer from Ebenezer Howard to Abercrombie.

19  J. M. Richards, *When we Build Again* (Architectural Press, 1942).
20  Jeff Daniels, 'Danspeak', *Autocar*, 6 July 1988.
21  Berthold Lubetkin, 'Town and Country Planning in Soviet Russia', *Architectural Association Journal*, 1932.
22  A confirmation of this helpless but not hopeless dependence was voiced by Professor Valery Legasov, leader of the Soviet delegation to the 1986 Vienna conference on the Chernobyl nuclear disaster:

Not only the Soviet Union but the rest of the world is dependent upon an expansion of nuclear energy. Without it any prospect of industrial growth after the year 2000 is a pious hope. The world of nuclear energy brings many dangers of an international character: transboundary releases of radiation, the proliferation of nuclear weapons, and international terrorism and the threat of damage to nuclear power plants in a time of war. The saturation of the world with so many types of dangerous industrial installations makes for conditions in which war is not permissible. (Reported in *The Times*, 26 August 1986)

# Bibliography

*Applied Science and Technological Progress*, a report to the committee on science and astronautics of the US House of Representatives by the National Academy of Sciences, Washington DC, 1967. See section by Charles Kimball, *Technology Transfer*.

Banham, Peter Reyner, *Theory and Design in the First Machine Age*, Architectural Press, London, 1960.

Banham, Peter Reyner, *The Architecture of the Well-tempered Environment*, Architectural Press, London, 1969.

Banham, Peter Reyner, *Design by Choice*, Academy Editions, London, 1981 (includes last reprint of 1965 essay, 'A Home is not a House').

Blake, Peter, *The Master Builders*, Gollancz, London, 1960.

Bowley, Marian, *Innovations in Building Materials*, Duckworth, London, 1960.

Carter, Peter, *Mies van der Rohe at Work*, Praeger, New York, 1974.

Caudill, William Wayne, *Architecture by Team*, Van Nostrand Reinhold, New York, 1971.

Collins, A. R. (ed.), *Structural Engineering: Two Centuries of British Achievement*, Tarot Print Ltd, London, 1983.

Comper, Sir J. N., *The Atmosphere of a Church*, Sheldon Press, London, 1947.

Conrads, Ulrich and Hans Sperlich, *Fantastic Architecture*, Architectural Press, London, 1963.

Cook, Peter, *Architecture: Action and Plan*, Studio Vista, London, 1967.

Crook, J. Mordaunt, *The Dilemma of Style*, John Murray, London, 1988.

Crosby , Theo, *Let's Build a Monument*, Pentagram, London, 1987.

Davies, Colin, *High Tech Architecture*, Thames & Hudson, London, 1988.

*Developments in the Structural Application of Light Gauge Galvanised Steel in Building*, Department of Civil Engineering, University of Surrey, 1979. See section 5.0: Nick Whitehouse, *The Matrex Frame*.

Eder, W. E. and W. Gosling, *Mechanical System Design*, Pergamon Press, Oxford, 1965.

Esher, Lionel, *The Broken Wave: The Rebuilding of Britain 1945–1970*, Allen Lane, London, 1981.

Forster, E. M., 'The Machine Stops', first published in the anthology *The Celestial Omnibus* in 1911. Penguin Books edition *Collected Short Stories* published in 1954.

Fry, E. Maxwell, *Fine Building*, Faber & Faber, London, 1944.

Fuller, Richard Buckminster, *Nine Chains to the Moon*, Lippincott, New York, 1938, and Southern Illinois University Press, Carbondale, 1963.

Fuller, Richard Buckminster, *Critical Path*, Hutchinson, London, 1983.

Fuller, Richard Buckminster, *The Buckminster Fuller Reader*, ed. James Meller, Jonathan Cape, London, 1970.

Gill, Brendan, *Many Masks: A Life of Frank Lloyd Wright*, Heinemann, London, 1988.

Gorer, Geoffrey, *The Life and Times of the Marquis de Sade*, Peter Owen, London, 1953.

Grove, Eric, *World War Two Tanks*, Orbis, London, 1976.

Hannon, B. M., R. G. Stein, B. Z. Segal, P. F. Deibert, M. Buckley and D. Nathan, *Energy Use for Building Construction*, Energy Research Group, Center for Advanced Computation, University of Illinois at Urbana Champaign; Richard G. Stein and Associates, New York, NY, CERDA Contract no. EY-76-S-02-2791, October 1977.

Hill, Canon D. Ingram, *Canterbury Cathedral*, Bell & Hyman, London, 1986.

Hudson, Liam, *Night Life: The Interpretation of Dreams*, Weidenfeld, London, 1986.

Jencks, Charles, *Modern Movements in Architecture*, Anchor Books, New York, 1973.

Jencks, Charles, *The Language of Postmodern Architecture*, Academy Editions, London, 1977.

Jencks, Charles and George Baird (eds), *Meaning in Architecture*, George Braziller, New York, 1969.

Kahn, Herman, *On Thermonuclear War*, Greenwood Press, London, 1978.

Kelly, Burnham, *The Prefabrication of Houses*, The Technology Press of the Massachusetts Institute of Technology and John Wiley and Sons Inc., New York, 1951.

Klotz, Heinrich, *The History of Post-Modern Architecture*, MIT Press, London, 1988.

Koenig, Giovanni K., 'How Car Design has Changed', *FIAT 1899–1989: An Italian Industrial Revolution*, Fabbri Editori, Turin, 1988.

Kopp, Anatole, *Constructivist Architecture in the USSR*, Academy Editions, London, 1985.

Landau, Royston, *New Directions in British Architecture*, Studio Vista, London, 1968.

Lane, Barbara Miller, *Architecture and Politics in Germany: 1919–1945*, Harvard University Press, 1968.

McDonald, Alan, *The Weller Way*, Faber & Faber, London, 1986.

Madge, John (ed.), *Tomorrow's Houses*, Pilot Press, London, 1946.

Mallory, Keith and Arvid Ottar, *The Architecture of Aggression: Military Architecture of Two World Wars*, Architectural Press, London, 1973.

Mann, Thomas, *Past Masters*, Martin Secker, London, 1933.

Morrison, Elting W., *Men, Machines and Modern Times*, MIT Press, Boston, 1966.

Nixon, St John C., *The Invention of the Automobile*, Country Life Books, London, 1936.

Norberg-Schultz, C., *Intentions in Architecture*, MIT Press, Boston, 1965.

Pawle, Gerald, *The Secret War*, Harrap, London, 1956.

Pawley, Martin, *The Private Future: Causes and Consequences of Community Collapse in the West*, Thames & Hudson, London, 1974.

Pawley, Martin, *Building for Tomorrow: Putting Waste to Work*, Sierra Club Books, San Francisco, 1982.

Pevsner, Nikolaus, *The Cathedrals of England*, Viking, London, 1985.

Propst, Robert, *The Office, A Facility Based on Change*, Herman Miller, New York, 1968.

Rabbit, Peter, *Drop City*, Olympia Press, New York, 1971.

Rand, Ayn, *The Fountainhead*, Norton, New York, 1943.

Rattray-Taylor, Gordon, *The Doomsday Book*, Thames & Hudson, London, 1970.

Richards, J. M., *When we Build Again*, Architectural Press, London, 1942.

Richards, J. M., *Architectural Criticism in the Nineteen Thirties*, Architectural Press, London, 1960.

Saint, Andrew, *The Image of the Architect*, Yale University Press, London, 1983.

Saint, Andrew, *Towards a Social Architecture*, Yale University Press, London, 1987.

Schon, Donald, *The Reflective Practitioner: How Professionals Think in Action*, Temple Smith, London, 1983.

Scruton, Roger, *The Aesthetics of Architecture*, Methuen, Cambridge, 1979.

Silver, Nathan and Jos Boys (eds), *Why is British Architecture so Lousy?*, Newman, London, 1980.

Spengler, Oswald, *The Decline of the West* (2 vols), translated by Charles Francis Atkinson, Alfred Knopf, New York, 1963.

Spengler, Oswald, *Man and Technics*, translated by Charles Francis Atkinson, Alfred Knopf, New York, 1963.

Wates, Nick and Charles Knevitt, *Community Architecture: How People are Creating their own Environment*, Penguin, London, 1987.

Whiffen, Marcus, *American Architecture since 1780*, MIT Press, Boston, 1969.

Yorke, F. R. S., *The Modern House*, Architectural Press, London, 1934.

Zuk, William and Roger Clark, *Kinetic Architecture*, Van Nostrand Reinhold, New York, 1970.

# Index

References to illustrations are given in **bold** type